WHOLE-HEARTED
PARENTING

How to use emotional intelligence to create
more peace, connection, and joy

Joshua Freedman

Copyright ©2016, Joshua Freedman

Published by Six Seconds

PO Box 1985

Freedom, CA 95019

Web: www.6seconds.org

Email: staff@6seconds.org

Phone: (831) 763-1800

Cover Design by Mark Lee

Library of Congress Control Number: 2015919001

ISBN: 978-1-935667-25-4

Printed in the USA

Dedication

To Emma and Max, thank you for letting me be your Daddy, and persevering to teach me how.

Thanks

Thank you to Karen McCown and Anabel Jensen for all the support and wisdom – many of the solutions in this book came from your counsel.

I'm very grateful to my editor, Elizabeth Dougherty, and to our Director of Parent Education, May Duong, for your support to bring the book to life.

As I explain in the book, many of the ideas here come from conversations with Six Seconds' team members around the world about the fun and challenges of parenting – thank you in particular to my colleagues who have shared these discussions about parenting with emotional intelligence: Marilynn Jorgensen, Sue McNamara, Max Ghini, Jayne Morrison, Lorenzo Fariselli, Jenny Wiley, Susan & Paul Stillman, Yoshimi Miyazaki, Marsha Rideout, Ilaria Boffa, Natalie Roitman, Maria Olsson, Cindy Handler, and many more I am sure. Please forgive me for not listing everyone!

CONTENTS

Introduction 9

The Cast of Characters. 14

What Is Emotional Intelligence?. 17

What's in this Book 22

Part I: Know Yourself 25

Chapter 1: Tuning into Emotions. 29

Enhancing Emotional Literacy 29

The Neuroscience of Emotion. 33

Chapter 2: Why Did I Do That? 45

The Process for Learning 47

Reacting to Feelings. 49

The Other Lesson: Praise and Criticism. 55

Chapter 3: Helping Kids with Self-Awareness 61

Enhancing Emotional Literacy 63

Teaching Children About Patterns 66

Discipline Strategies. 72

The Ugly Secrets of Parenthood: Wrapping Up Part I 75

Part II: Choose Yourself 79

Chapter 4: From Reaction to Response 87

Apply Consequential Thinking. 87

Perfectionism, Passivity, and Overprotection 93

Navigate Emotions 101

Chapter 5: Creating New Possibilities 109

Choosing a Role: Victim, Ally, or Dictator. 116

Fueling Your Internal Motivation 117

Exercise Optimism 121

Chapter 6: Helping Your Children Choose Themselves 127

Discipline Strategies and Time-Out 131

Whose Childhood Is It?. 137

Precious Feelings (or Max's Nap): Wrapping Up Part II. 143

Part III: Give Yourself 147

Chapter 7: From War To Peace – Increase Empathy. . 153

Paradigm of Facts, Force, or Fear. 154

Don't Just Do Something 157

Chapter 8: Choosing The Future - Pursue Noble Goals 163

When I Grow Bigger Bigger. 165

Orangutan Heart 166

Defining Your Noble Goal 168

Chapter 9: Teaching About Give Yourself 171

A Wish for Empathy. 173

Vision Alignment Activity. 176

Fourth-Grade *Satyagraha*. 183

Let Them Lead. 185

Chapter 10: The Cusp of Tomorrow 187

About The Author. 191

Invitation: Virtual Book Club. 193

About the Publisher. 193

Introduction

"

One does not discover new lands
without consenting to lose sight of the
shore for a very long time.

- Andre Gide

"

HELP WANTED!

I was a teacher years before being a parent. My students' parents would often ask my advice, and in the confidence of ignorance, I solemnly doled out answers. While I'd like to think some of my advice was useful, after having ridden the roller coaster of parenting for 16 years so far, I can now say with certainty: *I was an idiot*.

In this book, I will attempt to be less idiotic by giving less advice. When my wife, Patty, was pregnant and when our children were babies, she bought many parenting books. I didn't like them because most seem to say, "The way I've raised my children is right, and if you're a good parent you'll follow these rules." The underlying falsehood is that children are alike, and rational rules will work for any of them, anywhere.

My experience has been different. I find children to be more like ripples of sand on the shore. Beautiful, changing, complicated. Made of the same substance yet infinitely varied, and nearly impossible to shape into a predictable mold.

With that in mind, I'd like to start this book by saying: **I have no idea how you should parent *your* children**.

Instead I'd like to offer hundreds of tips and insights that can help you figure out your own answers. I am not a Parenting Expert. For the last 18 years I've helped lead Six Seconds, a nonprofit devoted to creating positive change around the world by teaching people how to use emotions more effectively. I've been privileged to work with many wise and compassionate people. On the way I've studied neuroscience and how the brain works – and attempted to apply that in my own parenting. This book is full of the insight that I wish I'd had when my two kids were small – now Emma is 16 and Max is 14, and I continue to wish for and seek out more skills to handle the complexities.

Parenting is filled with feelings. Sometimes I've wished to shut some emotions out, such as my kids' impatience with one another, or my own frustration with them. Yet studying about emotions, I've come to see we need a full range of feelings to learn, grow, and connect; it's a *whole-hearted* experience. While the joy and peace are easy to value, we also need the anger to tell us we've got a problem, and the sorrow to strengthen compassion. All our children's feelings, and all of ours, are present to help us tune in and grow.

This whole-hearted approach is based on *emotional intelligence*, sometimes called "EQ" for *emotional quotient* (a play on IQ for *intelligence quotient*). EQ simply means being smarter with feelings. It's blending our thinking and feeling to guide our actions with care – I'll explain this in more detail in a few pages.

I believe increasing emotional intelligence will enhance, even transform, your parenting to be more peaceful, collaborative, and joyful. As a result, at the core, this book is about understanding your own emotions and why you react the ways you do as a parent. It offers strategies for changing how you react in different situations, developing your emotional intelligence skills, and fostering those same skills in your children.

I illustrate these strategies mostly through stories – some of my prouder parenting moments and many of the times I've mucked it up. In 2004, I wrote a blog post called "Little Miss Bossy Pants." The struggle I faced then is probably why I ended up writing this book:

> By 9 a.m. I was ready to go back to bed. My head was ringing from near-constant explosions: the tyke battle zone.
>
> Emma Rose Freedman is five going on 45, CEO of the World. In my emotionally intelligent moments, she is *strong willed and dynamic*. At my wit's end, she is *bossy and volatile*.
>
> Emma has clear ideas about the way the world should be, and when someone disagrees, sometimes she snarls, yells, or otherwise explodes. She is incredibly frustrated when people won't do what she tells them to do. After all, it makes perfect sense to her. This appears as a total lack of patience... and, of course, I play right in by being impatient with her impatience.

I suspect part of my own frustration is my memory of being my sister's little brother. While I love her to pieces (now), she *still* likes to take charge (and the rest of us have learned we don't need to because she will).

When things calm down enough to talk, five-year-old-Emma recognizes, at least intellectually, that this behavior is not the way to win friends and influence people. But she's got this pattern well established already. In the heat of the moment Emma snaps into anger at the drop of a hat – or putting her plate in the wrong place, or moving her light without asking, or telling her to get dressed for school...

So, other than checking myself into an asylum, what do you advise? Have you faced and solved this problem? If so, how??? If not, what didn't work?

I received a ton of replies to this post, but unfortunately, no one had "the answer." I learned:

1) I'm not the only one facing this kind of challenge.

2) While there are no "solutions," there are a lot of options.

3) I have many opportunities to experiment and keep learning.

I hope this book provides those three elements for you.

THE CAST OF CHARACTERS

Sixteen years into this parenting adventure, my basic takeaway: This is the most exciting and powerful "project" I've ever imagined. True, many days I fail to live up to my own standards; I find it miraculous that my children are so wonderful. Despite the failings, I think Patty and I are good parents – and we're creating a family I find enchanting and delightful – at least most days.

Since the Emma and Max were little, I've traveled a lot. When they were both under five, I was on the road every other week. As do many, my wife deserves a medal for making it through that with her sense of humor intact. Patty is one of those people with 703 projects going on simultaneously. Often you can't quite walk through our house without dodging some marvelous creation she and the kids are creating. She was a fifth-grade teacher, the kind you remember your whole life. I imagine many of her students remember her as "the one who taught me I could do absolutely anything if I worked hard." We met in college and have been best friends for over half our lives.

A few years ago, we decided to take advantage of the frequent flyer miles and started home schooling. Airplane schooling? For five years, we took a few big trips a year, living in a part of the world for six to 12 weeks.

Along the way, Emma became an environmental activist and scientist. Near the end of our last big trip, when she was 14 years old, I watched her presenting to a group of Japanese parents and kids, teaching them about the effects of logging in the rainforest. Just a few years before, she'd been quite shy. (Typical of many academically gifted children, she's a perfectionist). Yet there, standing about the height of the adult Japanese women, it was clear she'd found her voice.

Like so many younger brothers, including me, Max enjoys just a little trouble. His favorite target, of course, is his uber-responsible big sister. He has some learning challenges that make activities like memorizing multiplication tables feel as easy as climbing Mt. Everest. Yet a couple years ago he learned how to build himself a computer, so he seems to be adapting. He loves being outside, and now he's teaching me to help him keep bees. He sees that without them the environment is in peril, and so it's a way of giving back (and the honey is delicious). He's a kid who lights up a room with his ready smile and genuine care.

I have both a personal and professional interest in this topic of parenting. As the CEO of Six Seconds, I lead a network of thousands of "emotional intelligence practitioners," trainers, consultants and coaches who have been accredited to use Six Seconds' methods and assessments in their work (ranging from internal leadership universities at multinational companies to individuals coaches). I travel internationally working with our offices and network members, many of whom are educators and parent educators. I research how to use EQ to create value and teach people how to measure and teach these skills in business, schools, government and other organizations.

On the personal side, over the last 16 years, I've "researched" this book by talking to parents from around 60 countries. In my speaking and writing, I find it's most useful to speak from my own experience, so I often find myself citing my experiences as a dad even when I'm talking about business leadership. One of my favorite aspects of this work is that people who are passionate about spreading emotional intelligence tend to be both caring and insightful. In turn, the work has helped me as a parent tremendously.

For example, one day when the kids were very young, I was teaching a workshop. That night, Patty was going away on a short trip. I said to my class, "I've got to get back home because I'm babysitting tonight and tomorrow." One of the trainees gave me a wonderful gift by challenging me: "When they're your own kids, it's called 'parenting,' not 'babysitting.'" Ouch, that was a powerful moment of self-awareness.

Conversations like these helped me realize that if I'm going to be worthy of the title "Daddy," I needed to reevaluate. It wouldn't be enough to show up as an occasional babysitter. Being a parent is something deeper. That shift to more active and conscious parenting is what this book is all about.

How can I, how can we, do that? Maybe emotions can help us. Feelings are signals. They indicate when we're on track, and when there's a problem. They nudge us toward being the parents we mean to be. This is the essence of whole-hearted parenting. On the other hand, if we are fighting with our own feelings, judging some as *good* and some as *bad*, it's going to be quite difficult to pick up those little nudges. As researcher and author Brené Brown says: *When you suppress any feelings, you suppress all feelings.* To access the energy and wisdom of emotion, we need a whole-hearted approach.

It's a lot easier to say it than to do it. But a lot of research about emotional intelligence and my own experience tell me it's possible. I'd summarize it like this:

Today is a chance to do better.

Every day, many times a day, we (parents and children) have the opportunity to learn together. Each of us can accept this invitation, or give into inertia and let the days fade into a routine. My advice is a simple lifelong challenge: **Capture those moments, grab hold with both hands, and with your *whole heart*, with courage and compassion, seize those intangible blossoms, thorns and all.**

How to do that? In large part, it's up to your own invention. If you enter each day with the conviction that you'll learn, there is no doubt that you will. That said, the book is full of tools and tricks to make this process a little smoother and a little more fruitful.

WHAT IS EMOTIONAL INTELLIGENCE?

Before we jump into the next part of the book, I'd like to explain a bit more about "emotional intelligence" and the structure of the book.

In this book, I use the terms *EQ* and *emotional intelligence* frequently and interchangeably. Here's what they mean:

> *EQ is an abbreviation for "Emotional Quotient," the measure of emotional intelligence (like IQ is a measure of cognitive intelligence).*
>
> *Emotional intelligence just means* ***being*** **smart with feelings.**

It's a pretty simple idea, really. We've all got feelings, and we can blunder along with them, or we can tune in and use them carefully. It may be helpful to consider the different between being smart *about* feelings, and smart *with* feelings. Emotions researchers are smart *about* feelings – they have knowledge. Being smart *with* feelings is different. This small shift is a powerful. EQ is a way to understand the nature of emotions and to use them as part of our intelligence, to apply the smarts to take effective action.

In 1997, a group of educators formed an organization to teach about EQ. We called it Six Seconds to capture the idea that emotional intelligence is something quick and easy – and because emotions actually last for only six seconds in our bodies. Emotions are neurotransmitters, chemical messengers that go into the blood stream, deliver their signals, and then are reabsorbed.

You are in the grocery store, your kid starts demanding you buy some crazy new cereal, and steam starts coming out your ears. You perceived an issue and started to produce chemical messengers to alert your body to prepare to combat this menace. The chemicals go flowing through your blood, and they carry messages to every living cell in your body. That whole process takes about six seconds.

We started Six Seconds because we could see that all over the world, people are working to create change, but getting stuck. Some changes require technical skills, but most often change stalls because of feelings and relationships. So we teach the skills of emotional intelligence to equip people to drive change – personally, professionally, and globally.

Six Seconds' mission is to support people to create positive change, everywhere, all the time. *Everywhere* means all around the world. *All the time* means in our daily lives. And *positive change* means taking a small step to make our lives and the world better.

Positive change might mean creating healthier relationships. Making companies where people can be and do their best. Developing thriving communities. Building schools where kids feel nourished and on fire with the joy of learning.

As parents, we have countless opportunities for positive change. Some are mundane: I'd like not to explode when I see my son trying to finish *today's* homework on the way out the door. Others are profound: I want my kids to grow up to be positive change-makers.

PARENTING WITH EMOTIONAL INTELLIGENCE

To make emotional intelligence into a practical, actionable process, we developed a model. It has three straightforward steps to help people be smarter with feelings:

1) **Be more aware.** Actively pay attention to emotions; they're messages.

2) **Be more intentional.** Pause and evaluate, so you can respond carefully instead of reacting automatically.

3) **Be more purposeful.** Take this present moment to move toward your future goal.

In the Six Seconds Model, we call these three steps *Know Yourself*, *Choose Yourself*, and *Give Yourself*, and it's a process anyone can use any time. It's especially useful when life gets complex. An example:

Becca is four, and she's decided she doesn't like wearing shoes. Joan, her mother, was up half the night with the baby and now needs to get Becca to school, the baby to daycare, and herself to work before her grumpy boss scolds her *again* for being late. Oh, and it's snowing.

If I were the parent, I suspect there would next be some shouting and tears, and a bad start to the day for everyone. How about you? Can you see a way to diffuse this bomb?

Fortunately, Joan has been practicing emotional intelligence and whole hearted parenting skills. Here's what might happen:

Know Yourself. Joan notices she's tired and impatient, and she knows her typical pattern when she feels impatient is to start pushing people. Her impatience is telling her there's an obstacle to overcome, but she realizes that Becca and shoes are not the real issue.

Choose Yourself. Joan clearly sees that her old way of reacting would lead to a bad experience for her and the kids. While she's short on time and energy, she has been practicing optimism, so she is certain that

The Six Seconds Model of Emotional Intelligence

she has options. Maybe she should take off her own shoes? Maybe they should all call in sick today? No, she's still not sure how to respond, but now she has become more curious than frustrated about how to solve the problem.

Give Yourself. Joan tries to tune into what her heart is saying to her, and realizes that for Becca, the shoe fight probably isn't the real issue and wonders if Becca is scared about going to school today. She remembers a quote she's posted on her bathroom mirror, something about finding celebration everywhere. She thinks about the lesson she would ideally like Becca to learn. Aha! She has it: It's time for Pookey Bunny to come to the rescue.

What ensues is a minute of Broadway-worthy theater: Joan in the role of Pookey Bunny who doesn't want to wear *any* clothes, and Becca who's trying to get Pookey to keep her clothes on and put on shoes. The whole episode takes under two minutes, and they laugh about it for years to come.

The story of Becca, Joan, and Pookey is fictional – but it's one I've heard a hundred times. You might be thinking, "My kids wouldn't fall for the Pookey Bunny routine," and, of course, they might not. I'm not suggesting that role-playing stuffed animals is a universal solution. Remember, I don't believe there's one answer that will fit all of our kids. The point is that by following these three steps, Joan shifted out of her old pattern and was able to think of something new and creative.

You might also be thinking, "Come on Josh, it's not that easy," and, of course, it's not. Joan's little moment of EQ is incredibly difficult. That small shift in perspective may be one of the most difficult things in life – the deck was stacked against her, and she had to overcome a lot of inertia. But it's possible. Can you imagine doing that yourself?

WHAT'S IN THIS BOOK

The rest of the book is organized into three parts that correspond with the three parts of the Six Seconds Model – Know Yourself, Choose Yourself, and Give Yourself. Each section has stories and information about emotional intelligence skills for us we can apply to parenting. Then there's a chapter with ideas and tools for sharing these skills with our children.

Part I - Know Yourself

What if we could tune in and see ourselves more clearly?

Why do we act the way we do? Why do our children? In this section, you'll learn more about emotions and how they fuel behavior.

We've all learned lessons about how to cope with life's challenges and, as a result, react in a certain ways over and over. Some of those learned ways are invaluable, but others are not worth continuing. If we could see ourselves more clearly, it would make it easier for sort the dross from the good stuff.

Part II - Choose Yourself

How can we more thoughtfully do more of what we actually mean to do?

Yes, we've all learned certain ways of reacting, but maybe we don't *have* to follow those patterns. This section is about skills for being more intentional.

We're all physically wired to react to protect ourselves from stress and threat. But we also have some choice about what we do when we react. If we can develop more skills to exercise that choice, we can learn to respond with care and intention instead.

Part III - Give Yourself

What if we could each see our own vision of the future more clearly and use that to inform our parenting?

All this is hard work – what will drive us to continue? This section is about using empathy and purposeful intent to support ourselves to take more optimal actions.

One of the most powerful ways of getting out of defensive reactions is to remember: There's something more important than being right. These tools help us look to the long term and approach parenting with compassion and clarity.

Lather, Rinse, Repeat

In the Six Seconds Model, we depict the three steps in a circle to remind ourselves that it's a process – Know Yourself, Choose Yourself, Give Yourself, repeat. Each time we move through the three steps, we can be more effective as we create peace and joy with our children. In the rough spots, we might need to go through the cycle many times to reach a positive resolution.

As we go around and around this process, we're more and more able to use our whole hearts to make optimal choices.

The Skills of Emotional Intelligence

When you studied math in school, you learned some techniques, such as simplifying equations. This technique helped you solve many different types of math problems. In other words, it helped you put your mathematical intelligence into action.

Likewise, there are specific, learnable, measurable techniques to help you put your emotional intelligence into action. We refer to these techniques as *competencies*, and throughout the book, I'll explain them in terms of parenting, why they matter, and how they work. The table on the next page lists the competencies associated with each of the three steps in the Six Seconds Model, along with the benefit and a definition. The structure of the book maps to the three steps, and each of the competencies is described in the book.

Step	Competency	Benefit	Definition
KNOW YOURSELF	**Enhance emotional literacy**	Awareness	Accurately identifying and understanding feelings. Page 29
	Recognize patterns	Insight	Acknowledging frequently recurring reactions and behaviors. Page 45
CHOOSE YOURSELF	**Apply consequential thinking**	Integrity	Evaluating the costs and benefits of your choices. Page 87
	Navigate emotions	Balance	Assessing, harnessing, and transforming emotions as a strategic resource. Page 101
	Engage intrinsic motivation	Passion	Gaining energy from personal values and commitments vs. being driven by external forces. Page 109
	Exercise optimism	Innovation	Taking a proactive perspective of hope and possibility. Page 121
GIVE YOURSELF	**Increase empathy**	Connection	Recognizing and appropriately responding to others' emotions. Page 153
	Pursue noble goals	Purpose	Connecting your daily choices with your overarching sense of purpose. Page 163

Now that you have this map of the book, let's jump into the first step: Know Yourself. In this chapter we'll look at challenges like, "Why can't I get this #*$@ car seat to work?" And bigger questions such as: What does it mean to be a parent?

PART I

Know Yourself

What if we could tune in and see ourselves more clearly?

In Part I:

Introduction: Where Are this Child's Parents?

Chapter 1: Tuning into Emotions

> **Enhance emotional literacy**: Name and understand feelings.

Chapter 2: Why Did I Do That?

> **Recognize patterns**: Notice and acknowledge recurring reactions.

Chapter 3: Helping Kids with Self-awareness

INTRODUCTION:

Where Are this Child's Parents?

Around 9 p.m. on a Spring night, my wife, Patty, went into labor. Time slowed to minutes between contractions. Then the drive to the hospital two minutes at a time, two miles at a time. It was as if all that mattered in the world was contained in this small space.

Early the next morning, time slowly began again. At 4:56 a.m., Emma was born. The first second. Then the next second. Her first breath. Our first touch. A whole life of wonder and possibility as we gazed at her.

Gradually, seconds turned into minutes. She was ten minutes old. Ten minutes new. There is so much packed into those minutes, noticing every breath, every tiny wrinkle. Before long, an hour had passed, and soon several hours. Time slowly sped up. When people asked, "How old is your baby" we first measured in days, then weeks, then months. Now years, and soon decades.

What happens to all those seconds? What happens to those whole lifetimes we could live between heartbeats? Each moment will never come again, each moment made precious because it is now, here, real, alive. How can we as parents exult in these moments?

At first, parenthood was so intense that I just dove in and didn't think about the next steps. Despite being tired and groggy, I felt so alive. Yes, stupid-bone-tired, but enchanted.

My wife and I looked at our daughter, and it took nothing to bring tears welling up, our hearts overflowing with wonder and wishes, with hopes and fears – in love with not only Emma but with life. In those days, it was so easy to see that life is miraculous. Together as a family we are a miracle. I was so proud to be a part of it, to feel it.

From that sense of wonder and hope, I found the journey got increasingly confusing. I remember a few days later with an incessantly shrieking child, thinking, "Where the #@*& are this child's parents to take care of her?" Then the cold finger of realization that it was our job.

The first time I left Patty and the baby home to take a nap and went to work for a couple hours, I came home to both of them wide awake and inconsolable. "I thought you were going to take a nap?" I asked. Patty's ironic reply, between sobs, "This is how we nap."

Two years later Max was born, and I was able to reconnect to that sense of miracle. And life got even more complex.

I never could have anticipated just how many choices we would have to make as parents. And not just about what brand of diaper to buy or how to secure the damn car seat. I find the most challenging choices are not about what I should *do*, but about who I want to *be*. There are so many decisions to negotiate, and so many emotions attached to them.

I wish I could hold onto that feeling of limitless possibility. Yet in the day-to-day struggles, I find myself reacting with impatience and judgment. Some days, however, I find enough clarity to notice those problematic reactions before they come to a boil. Early detection is key, which is why the first two competencies – *enhance emotional literacy* and *recognize patterns* – in the Six Seconds Model are so valuable. Both competencies support the first step: Know Yourself. I'll talk about emotional literacy in chapter 1 and recognizing patterns in chapter 2.

These skills help us know ourselves. From this foundation of self-awareness, we gain clarity: *I can now see what I'm doing.* Then later, we can choose if that's what we want to be doing.

Chapter 1: Tuning into Emotions

The field of neuroscience is exploding, and researchers are learning more and more every day about how our brains work.

Emotions are part of our basic biology. We can pretend to be rational and ignore our own and others' feelings, but that's actually irrational, because emotions are central to the way our brains function. Emotions are a core survival function, and they cannot be turned off.

On the other hand, if we don't fight our emotions and instead focus on them as something useful, we can get incredible insight about ourselves as parents and about our children. The process of developing emotional literacy begins by considering that emotion is something worth our attention.

Next we can get more accurate in naming and understanding emotions. The research on this is fascinating: Simply naming our own feelings alters our emotional state. Saying to yourself, for example, "I'm angry" has the power to dissipate the feeling and soothe you when you're angry. I like this little phrase as a reminder: "Name it to tame it." When you identify a feeling connected to stress and challenge and give words to your experience, the feeling begins to subside.

ENHANCING EMOTIONAL LITERACY

Emotional literacy, the first competency in the Six Seconds Model, is the ability to name and understand emotions. I feel happy because my child and I are going for a walk. I feel sad because I won't see my family for a week. As we enhance emotional literacy, we become more accurate and skilled at detecting and identifying emotions, even when they're subtle or complex.

When our kids are young, their emotions are pretty obvious. Little kids laugh out loud, shout, cry – they communicate what they feel. Parents are also full of feelings, and we communicate our emotions to our children. That's fun and beautiful on some days, but not so fun on more challenging days and in time of conflict.

People sometimes call emotions like anger and fear "negative" or "bad" feelings, but I believe feelings are just part of us. They're not good or bad. As we'll see when we soon talk about the neuroscience of emotions, feelings carry information and energy. What we do with that information and energy could be good or bad. Feelings are like electricity. Electricity is dangerous. If you put a fork in the electrical outlet, it can even kill you. But that doesn't mean electricity is bad, it means we need to learn about it and use it carefully.

If you're in a situation where you're angry at your child, it's a message that you see a problem. That's valuable information – it's a message from you, to you, saying: "Hey! Something isn't working."

This is at the core of whole-hearted parenting. Instead of thinking of some emotions as *good* and others as *bad*, consider that they're all data. They're signals that give us a little push to cope with challenges and seek out opportunities. As we're working to know ourselves better, we need a nonjudgmental approach. It's time to get more curious about our own reactions.

Making Friends with Feelings

Did you see *Inside Out*, the animated movie that personifies and explores feelings? If not, put it in your queue to learn about current research on emotions in an entertaining way. One of the most important steps to learning more about your feelings is to make friends with them. If you're telling yourself that your feelings are bad and confusing and overwhelming, then you are not going to want to spend time learning about them.

When I was younger, I tried not to think about feelings because I found them confusing and scary. During an acting class in college, my teacher, Marie, kept asking me how I was feeling. I was sad and scared because I was far away from the people I loved. One day I told her I didn't like thinking so much about feelings because I thought I might drown in all the feelings. She said, "I'm not asking you to jump into the water, just to put your toe in it."

That was a turning point for me. I experimented with Marie's advice, and I was surprised to learn that I could notice my feelings and tune into them without being overwhelmed by them. I could get closer to my own feelings instead of hiding from them. I could dip my toe in the water, and it was interesting, not dangerous. I still didn't understand feelings, but they were getting less scary.

Then I had children, and I had lots of feelings to grapple with! Mine, theirs, my spouse's. Just when I thought I was getting a handle on emotions, bam! Change happens, and we need to adapt.

The Rules of Emotions

Do you play chess? For someone who doesn't know the rules, it's confusing. Why do some pieces go one step, and some jump, and some zoom around in diagonals or lines? We could look at a chess game and say, "This is stupid – it makes no sense" and push it away. Or we could look at the apparent chaos and consider, "What rules govern this game?" Then we can play.

My colleague David Caruso uses chess as a metaphor: "Feelings are like chess pieces; there are certain moves they make."

Feelings don't just happen. There is logic behind them, and there are rules we can apply. This surprises many people. Personally, this insight has helped me be less afraid of feelings – my own and other people's.

Here are three rules I've learned:

1. Emotions get more or less intense.

Every basic emotion, such as joy or sorrow, fear or trust, can start out small and get bigger. A tiny bit of joy is peace. As we add more and more intensity, it might become contentment, then happiness, then delight, and even bliss.

If your child is a little anxious, and you scold him for not doing a good job, his anxiety will probably escalate to fear.

Imagine feelings like paints – each color has many subtle shades.

2. Emotions combine.

We usually experience many feelings simultaneously. Maybe you're taking your baby on her first airplane trip. You feel happiness about being together, anticipation that your parents are meeting the baby for the first time, worry that the baby might cry the whole flight, sad that your sister can't join you. That's a lot of feelings all at once.

Back to the paint metaphor: Colors combine.

These overlapping emotions makes it hard to sort out what we're feeling. Sometimes we name different combinations with a new word. If I'm feeling happiness and anticipation at the same time, we might call that *excitement*. If I'm feeling a little afraid and sad, that could be *vulnerable*.

3. Emotions focus our attention.

We have feelings because something is happening – something inside or something outside. For example, maybe your kid is playing soccer and he boots the ball way down the field, and you feel proud. That feeling is helping you remember to pay attention and remember this moment.

Maybe you made a resolution to take better care of yourself by exercising, and you haven't followed through. Maybe you're feeling frustrated and guilty. Those feelings are messages to remind you that you're not doing what you meant to do.

Those colorful paints are highlighting moments of our lives so that we pay attention. Emotions provide the spark and insight to help us whole-heartedly engage in the moments of our lives.

THE NEUROSCIENCE OF EMOTION

I'm fascinated by science behind emotional intelligence. As a person who values logic, studying *neurobiology* (the study of how brain cells affect our behavior) has helped me make more sense of my feelings, and my children's.

At a neurobiological level, emotions are chemicals. Technically they're *neurohormones*, molecules made of chains of proteins called *peptides*. Each neurohormone has a unique structure (like a key). These molecules are key to survival because they are messengers that help regulate our brains and bodies to cope with opportunities and threats.

When a child perceives a problem (*My little brother took my toy*), she will respond with feelings such as anger and frustration. The feelings push her to actions that might solve the problem (getting a parent to help) or might create new problems (grabbing the toy away).

The neurohormones of emotion carry information and energy. They are messengers that help regulate every living cell in our bodies. These chemicals are primarily produced in our brains, but the same chemicals are created all around our bodies, especially around the heart, gut, and spine. They form a kind of chemical messenger system between the brain and other body parts. In an open-loop feedback cycle, messages go back and forth. It's important to note that the emotions of other people strongly influence the signals.

So when my sweet seven-year-old-boy would slip his hand into mine as we walked down the street, his emotions and actions affected me. My body would start filling up with emotion chemicals. These messenger chemicals would flow from my body to mind, back and forth, helping me pay attention: to notice how happy I feel that my son wants to hold my hand, and savor the moment. In turn, my behavior might affect him. Holding my hand might make him feel happy too, maybe safe and secure as well. Emotions connect us.

Holding my hand might make him feel happy too, maybe safe and secure as well.

Emotions connect us.

The chemicals of emotion are completely mixed together with the chemicals of reason. We cannot separate logic and leave the emotion out of it. As neuroscientist Antonio Damasio said, "Emotions are enmeshed in the neural networks of reason."

In other words, the idea that we could *just leave emotions out of it* is a biological impossibility. Emotions are an integral part of how people function. So, we might as well learn what they are, and how to handle them.

Emotions, Feelings, and Moods

A basic emotion is an automatic physiological response to a stimulus. Emotions are produced primarily in the *hypothalamus*, a kind of factory in our brains that assembles these strings of protein as needed. When we perceive something, like our child's face, it takes about a quarter of a second for our brain to interpret the signal ("She's sad"), and about another quarter of a second to create the chemicals (the neurohormones that will carry the emotion message). The brain then releases the neurotransmitters, which go into the blood stream and affect our heart rate, muscles, and all our systems, so that we can react to the stimulus. Your baby cries; you register that she's upset. You want to comfort her; you pick her up.

The whole process of creating and using the chemicals could be quite fast (just over a half of a second) or it could take a few seconds. The molecules of emotion last for around six seconds before they're all absorbed. Then we produce more.

I often use the words emotion and feeling interchangeably, and usually that's fine. When we're working to know ourselves and digging into the nuance of these experiences, it may help to be more precise. Emotions come first, they're the immediate chemical reaction. Then feelings come from processing the emotion. The chemicals that make up the emotion affect us physically; as we begin to experience that, we feel something. Our muscle tension changes, our body temperature changes – after a few moments, as we internalize the experience, we have a *feeling*.

Along the emotional continuum, we also have *moods*, which are semi-persistent states. A mood is not connected to a specific stimulus but results from a series of experiences and feelings. For example, if we have a fun day with the kids at the park, there's laughter and play (and not much fighting), lunch was nice... these might add up to a good mood.

If we're eating and sleeping well, our relationships are healthy, and we're firing on all cylinders, we tend to be in a good mood. A good mood is a generalized signal of thriving and a message to keep going in this direction. When we're in a bad mood, we're more reactive and impatient. We're more likely to pay closer attention to obstacles that we perceive as being in the way of achieving what we want. We're also more likely to interpret new information in that light – so when in a grumpy mood, an unenthusiastic comment from a child might be treated as if it were a big act of defiance. Mood is highly affected by physical conditions, such as exercise, diet, lighting, and temperature, and mood becomes a kind of meta-filter that changes our emotional reactions.

Here's a scenario: You and the kids had a good night's sleep, ate a healthy breakfast, and now you're out at the park. You're in a pleasant mood. Then one child loses her sunglasses. When she notices they're gone, she is sad (emotion signaling loss) and begins to experience remorse (feeling signaling a problematic behavior). However, because of your pleasant mood, the news doesn't upset you as much as it would if you were tired and hungry. You comfort her, tell her she can earn the money to buy a new pair, and you all continue with your picnic.

DECODING THE MESSAGES

At a core level, emotions are a mechanism to help us cope and thrive as social animals. Different scientists have different theories to define the basic emotions. Robert Plutchik, a researcher who studied animal behavior and the role of emotions in survival, identified eight basic emotions that each has a physiological function. Based on Plutchik's work, here is my interpretation of the way the emotions help us:

Basic Emotion	Why We Have It
Anger	To fight against problems
Anticipation	To look forward and plan
Disgust	To reject what is unhealthy
Fear	To protect us from danger
Joy	To remind us what's important
Sadness	To connect us with those we love
Surprise	To focus us on new situations
Trust	To connect with people who help

For example, your child goes away to summer camp for a month. You feel sad as a reminder: *Hey! You love this kid. Take care of that relationship.* She's promised to write, so you go to the mailbox every day with anticipation: *Something interesting is going to happen.* Two weeks go by without a letter, and you feel anger: *This is* not *ok, and I'm going to make sure she knows it.*

Emotion Puzzles

These basic emotions combine into thousands of variations. There are around 3,000 different words for feelings in English to express a wide range of nuance. As we become more accurate in understanding this hidden language, we also increase our sense of emotional mastery. I've never seen a recipe book for all the feelings, but this table shows some ideas of how different emotions could combine to create some common feelings.

Feeling	Possible Recipe
Boredom	Disgust (rejection) + sadness (loss) + fear (risk)
Disappointment	Sadness (loss) and anger (there is a problem)
Hope	Anticipation (looking ahead) + joy (wants fulfilled)
Impatience	Anger (there is a problem) + anticipation (looking ahead)
Jealousy	Anger (there is a problem) + disgust (rejection) + fear (risk)
Loneliness	Sadness (loss) + fear (risk) + disgust (rejection)
Respect	Trust (accepting) + joy (wants fulfilled) + anticipation (looking ahead)
Worry	Fear (danger) + anticipation (looking ahead)

One reason for learning about emotions is for you to understand yourself better. Another, as I'll explain in the third chapter, "Helping Kids to Be More Self-aware," is so that you can help your children understand their emotions.

USEFUL EMOTIONS

The way I'm encouraging you to think about emotions could be called an *adaptive* approach. Researchers in the adaptive tradition see that emotions are part of our survival: They help us. Often the help is confusing because emotions don't hold up a sign saying, "Stop being an idiot and apologize to your child." Rather they give us a general sense that something is, or is not, going as desired. We combine this emotional sense with our cognitive intelligence to reach a good decision. That's emotional intelligence – being smart with feelings.

In other words: When we tune into the signal from an emotion and process that signal so that we understand what it means, we can then solve problems.

All emotions can help us in this process – it doesn't work to cherry-pick, accepting some emotions and rejecting others. Even feelings that seem problematic (such as anger) can help us.

Anger, for example, is a signal that our pathway is blocked. Imagine your child wants to join the debate team, and you're thrilled she's confident enough to take a risk and try something new that will challenge her. You overhear Aunt Marge telling her that would be too hard. You might feel angry. Your anger is a message: Something's in the way. In this case, it's Aunt Marge and her pessimism. The anger serves to focus your attention on the threat and motivates you to respond by fighting or pushing through the obstacle.

That's useful. Even a so-called-negative emotion like anger has a purpose. Now if you misheard Marge and tell her to back off, and your whole reaction is based on a mistake, it's a problem. Or if you say horrible things to Marge that you then regret, maybe you're overreacting. The usefulness of the anger depends also on the appropriateness of the thoughts and actions that follow it.

As Aristotle wrote:

> *Anybody can become angry – that is easy, but to be angry with the right person and to the right degree and at the right time and for the right purpose, and in the right way – that is not within everybody's power and is not easy.*

Emotions Focus and Motivate

As I've said, emotions are signals. They focus our attention on an opportunity or threat. In addition, emotions motivate us. They push us to deal with the opportunity or threat. In simple terms, emotions motivate us to move *toward* or *away* from something. Anger usually motivates us to move toward a problem; fear usually motivates us to back away.

Expanding Plutchik's eight basic emotions, we can consider a likely focus and motivation provided by each:

Basic Emotion	Focus	Motivation
Anger	Problem	Fight or push through
Anticipation	Opportunity	Move toward
Disgust	Problem	Reject
Fear	Threat	Protect
Joy	Opportunity	Do more of this
Sadness	Loss	Stop and clarify
Surprise	Uncertainty	Stop and look
Trust	Safety	Connect with others

Accepting Emotions

The best way to learn about feelings is to observe and discuss them. In my experience, kids provide *plenty* of opportunities for this! We can study our children and notice how their feelings operate. Of course, we can study our own feelings too. As a starting point, assume all feelings, yours and theirs, are present for a legitimate reason.

Your child is crying about losing a toy. Instead of dismissing it because it was inexpensive and not-very-special anyway, consider: The sorrow is teaching her to be more careful.

Your child is loudly joyful about friends coming to play. Instead of being frustrated by the volume, consider: The joy is teaching him the importance of friendship.

It's much easier with feelings such as hope, love, and compassion – but if we are practicing whole-hearted parenting, we will value all feelings. Some behavior is negative and should not be accepted, but the feeling is there for a reason.

This is a key point going back to the adaptive tradition. If emotions are present to help us survive and thrive, then we need to treat emotions as something useful.

Your three-year-old leaves his stuffed doggy at the park and is disconsolate. You could say, "Knock it off. It's only a dumb stuffed animal." Most parents wouldn't do that though because it's easy to see why he's so sad. You can see that the sorrow is legitimate, and we assess there was no ill intent involved.

On the other hand, a few years later the same child is breaking his pencil because, "This math homework is so stupid." A parent might tell him, "Knock it off. Just do your math." Why? Because the child's frustration is an obstacle to getting done what the parent needs the child to do, whether the child likes it or not. Ever find yourself saying to your child: "In the amount of time that you've spent complaining, you could have finished [fill in the blank]?" Instead what if we consider that our child is expressing a legitimate feeling? Maybe it would be more constructive if a parent took the time to find out why the child is struggling with math and look for ways to support him. In other words, rather than focusing on the symptom (the behavior), emotional intelligence helps us look for the underlying cause.

Rather than focusing on the symptom (the behavior), emotional intelligence helps us look for the underlying cause.

Feelings ≠ Actions

While a feeling might have a healthy, valuable message, it can also provoke destructive behavior. This is an essential point: **Thoughts, feelings, and actions are different**. We can feel angry, which is a useful signal that we have a problem, but we can act on that feeling in many ways. Some of the actions will help the situation; others won't. Breaking the pencil doesn't help address the underlying issue with the math (which could be a lack of understanding, or that it's too easy or too hard, or maybe the child would rather be playing Minecraft).

As parents, we can look at a situation and blur these together: *He is not doing a good job at math, and he needs to stop being angry and just do the work.* On the other hand, our emotional intelligence can help us be more precise. When we differentiate the feelings, thoughts, and actions, we can accept and value the feeling *and* help the child find a more appropriate action.

In the realm of emotional intelligence, one of the biggest mistakes people make is confusing thoughts, feelings, and actions. I might say to your child, "I feel like you're not listening to me," but that's a statement of *thought*. This inaccurate assertion might cause me to miss the important point that I *feel* hurt, or sad, or disrespected. When we blur thoughts–feelings–actions together into a big muddle, it's nearly impossible to gain the insight feelings can offer.

Accuracy is a key ingredient. When we're being mathematically intelligent, we're accurate with numbers. Using emotional intelligence helps us be accurate with feelings.

To understand your own emotional patterns as a parent, it will be invaluable to begin to differentiate these as three separate components:

> *Thoughts* are how we're evaluating. What we're telling ourselves.

> *Feelings* are what we're sensing. Our visceral experience.

> *Actions* are what we're doing. How we're behaving.

Tip: Almost all feelings can be expressed in one word. Sad. Joyful. Despairing. Exuberant. Silly. When we need a whole phrase, we're probably expressing a thought.

This process of self-observation is key to knowing yourself – and to using your whole heart as a parent. Remember to be curious about yourself rather than judgmental – it's not about getting an A, it's about self-discovery. As you continue to observe thoughts, feelings, and actions you might notice that there are certain combinations that recur. This is the start of recognizing patterns, the next EQ competency in the Six Seconds Model.

Chapter 2:
Why Did I Do That?

I remember a horrible moment 14 years ago. I was trying to get Emma to take a bath. She was resisting and fighting, or maybe I was the one resisting and fighting. Finally, I picked her up to put her in the tub. Little arms flailing, she hit me right on the nose, and I was infuriated. I said something incoherent, lifted her high in the air, and raised my arm to hit her back.

Fortunately, I saw myself.

Just for a moment, I saw this big enraged adult holding a tiny naked two-year-old, ready to smack her. I put her down and ran out of the room.

Over the years, Emma and I have had our share of tempests, but that incident was the closest I've come to really hitting her. It's painful for me to think about it. I feel disgust (rules violated) and sad (loss of love) to see that I am someone who could be so violently angry at someone so helpless.

In these moments of total failure as a parent, it's easy for me to get into self-blame. *Who am I to write about emotional intelligence for other parents when I need to get my own act together?* When I see in myself this kind of explosiveness and reactivity, I question my own integrity. That is not who I want to be. I try to remind myself: *Tomorrow I can do better.* I'm learning every day, and mistakes are part of the process.

This is a powerful way to see ourselves as parents. We are here to learn and to model this for our kids. Learning includes making mistakes and trying again. We don't expect our kids to instantly be good at long division. Every skill, including parenting, takes practice. In learning, a wrong answer is just as useful as a right answer – the process is what matters. When we get it wrong, it means that it's time to try again. This doesn't excuse all behavior, of course. Yet the vast majority of us have the opposite problem: We are overly self-critical.

> "
>
> When we observe ourselves in action, we can collect data. This is part of the journey of learning.
>
> "

THE PROCESS FOR LEARNING

To help ourselves learn be better parents, we need to practice, and we need data – feedback – about how effectively our experiments are working. Fortunately, we have hundreds, thousands, possibly millions, of opportunities to experiment. Every day when we're interacting with our children, it's another chance to watch ourselves in action. In some ways it doesn't matter if it's an EQ train wreck or a super-parent moment: When we observe ourselves in action, we can collect data. This is part of the journey of learning.

Self-observation gives you insight into your reactions and can inform what you choose to do in the future. Fortunately or not, a child is source of continuous feedback. Think about a typical day in your household and then try to step back, look for patterns, and note your behavior and feelings.

For example, mornings tend to be stressful times for many families. There is a lot to juggle as several family members need to get fed, dressed, and out the door on time. This makes it a prime chance to learn about ourselves in a moment of stress.

Think about how your morning went by asking yourself questions, such as: Was it a typical morning? How did your child respond to you? Is that the response you want? If not, what happened? How did you behave? What were you thinking and feeling right before that behavior? How did you react in that moment? Is that a recurring reaction of yours?

As we observe ourselves in the process of learning, it's useful to recognize that our interactions are not still pictures, they're little movies. A reaction doesn't just happen all at once, it's a sequence of small interactions combined. Imagine that you can rewind the video of a recent interaction with your child and see your own reaction building in slow motion, like a snowball rolling bigger and faster down a hill.

At Six Seconds, we call this process *recognizing patterns*. This competency involves noticing our own typical reactions. Seeing how our thoughts, feelings, and actions frequently flow together in ways that become predictable.

Coming back to neuroscience for a moment: Our brains love to form and follow patterns. It makes our brains efficient. It's easier and faster. If we had to carefully evaluate every moment of every day, it would be exhausting. Our brains form patterns to make it easier.

We all learn and reinforce patterns over time. They're like little scripts, like subroutines in computer programming. We practice them until we're highly efficient at following the patterns. Being able to see the patterns we've learned is key to being able to assess and change the patterns in the present.

> "
>
> The feeling doesn't create the thought or the action, but the feeling does influence them.
>
> "

REACTING TO FEELINGS

In order to recognize a pattern, we have to become skilled at identifying its ingredients: thoughts, feelings, and actions. Once we identify the ingredients, we can put them into a sequence and see how the pattern starts and how it unfolds.

Imagine your child is goofing around at breakfast. You say, "Settle down," but he continues his behavior. Maybe you feel impatient and wonder, "Is he ever going to learn to listen?" Somehow he ends up knocking over the milk, which careens into a bowl of Cheerios, which splashes into your coffee cup making a tsunami of cereal and milk and coffee, which ends up on your favorite shirt. (Don't even try to tell me it could never happen.) You know this is because he's impulsive and doesn't listen. You shout something you regret, slam your hand down on the table, and in the stunned silence you can't decide which is worse, the ruined shirt or the fact that you missed the chance to laugh with your kid about the new Cheerio-polka-dot fashion he's created.

Now let's go back through that story and tease apart the feelings, thoughts, and actions.

> **Thoughts**: He's goofing around. He doesn't listen. He's never going to learn. He's irresponsible. He's impulsive.

> **Feelings**: Impatient. Anxious/afraid. Stressed. Angry (outraged!). Regretful.

> **Actions**: Tell him to settle down. Glare. Shout. Slam hand on table.

The three are related but different. A *thought* is an assessment or interpretation. A thought doesn't create a feeling, but it does influence it. A *feeling* is just a feeling – a sensation. The feeling doesn't create the thought or the *action*, but the feeling does influence them. Consider: You could have the same feeling, the same thought, and a completely different action.

While there are many ways of responding to each situation, most of us tend to use one reaction over and over. If this shouting scenario is familiar, then you know that in a way, it feels good to get mad and shout. We do that, and we like *something* about it, and we do it again. We *know* that's not the best solution, but pretty soon it seems to happen automatically. Of course it's not. Behavior is something we learned in the past and reinforce by practicing – by using it over and over until it's easy and feels automatic.

Sometimes it's easier to notice other people's patterns. For example, do you know people who tend to blow up when they're mad? Or people who get very quiet when they're upset? Or people who leave the room to get away from an uncomfortable situation?

How about you?

How do you usually react when you're sad? Do you tend to shut down, get mad and blame someone, pretend not to be sad, make a joke, or something else?

What's your usual reaction when you're happy? Do you enjoy it, worry it won't last, or overreact or underreact?

How do you usually react when you're mad? Do you shout, take it out on someone else, glare, silently brood, or something else?

Now add your partner and kids to the mix, and it's even more complicated.

Sorting Out Thoughts, Feelings, and Actions

To practice this part of emotional intelligence, I highly recommend that you keep a journal or logbook. Review two moments of your day – one that didn't go well, one that did. For each moment, make a chart like the one on the next page, and use it to sort out your thoughts, feelings, and actions.

Remember a challenging moment from your day and try it now.

Situation: Cheerio-tsunami

Thoughts	Feelings	Actions
He's goofing around.	Impatient.	Tell him to settle down.
He doesn't listen.	Anxious/afraid.	
He's never going to learn.	Stressed.	Glare.
	Angry (outraged!).	Shout.
He's irresponsible.	Regretful.	Slam hand on table.
He's impulsive.		

Tips:

- To notice your thoughts, pay attention to what you are telling yourself. What's the tape looping in your own head?

- To tune into your feelings, notice your physical sensations. What parts of your body are tense, hot, painful? What is your own facial expression?

- To identify your actions, imagine a video camera watching the scene. What would it see and hear?

Your turn!

Situation:

Thoughts	Feelings	Actions

The next step is to consider a thought, feeling, or action that led you to the next thought, feeling, or action. You're working to identify a sequence, or chain of events. Articulate them in this template:

> *When (<u>stimulus</u>), I (<u>typical reaction</u>).*

For example, here are some patterns I often follow:

- When I feel angry, I shout.

- When I feel grateful, I connect.

- Often when I think someone is interested, I feel committed.

- When I am hungry, I am impatient.

- When I feel curious, I look more carefully.

- When I think someone isn't listening, I feel hurt.

- When I feel helpless, I assert power.

As I mentioned, it may be easier to see another person's patterns. I suspect that if your children are more than a handful of years old, it will be pretty easy for you to see how they typically react. For example, what do they usually do when they don't get their way? When Max thinks someone is criticizing him, he blames others. When Emma is uncertain, she shuts down.

Think about your child, spouse, or close relative: What does that person do when someone says *no* to him/her? How about when receiving a compliment? In a social situation with new people?

As you begin to see other people's patterns, it might help you notice your own.

Patterns Combine

One of the big challenges is that we reinforce one another's patterns. It's very easy to see between siblings or partners. One of my son's patterns: *When I think someone is trying to control me, I provoke.* One of my daughter's: *When I feel anxious, I assert control.* You can imagine that the two of them provoke one another's patterns. Probably, they taught these patterns to each other.

Of course, many of our children's patterns come from us. Sometimes they pick up patterns that we model. Sometimes they create patterns in opposition to our patterns. As you start to see patterns of your family members, you can also start to consider: What is my part in their pattern?

This is a big challenge. When your child is behaving in a way that you dislike, it's much easier to blame the child, or your partner, or the media, but blaming anyone (including yourself) won't effect change. Instead, get curious. Look at the child's behavior and ask yourself: *What pattern is he following?* Then, the hard part: *What pattern of mine is reinforcing his pattern?*

For example, young Ali is throwing tantrums left and right. Beth, her mom, observes and identifies that Ali's pattern is: *When I feel lonely, I have a tantrum.*

Then mom has an aha! moment: Beth realizes that she reacts to tantrums by giving Ali lots of attention: *When I perceive a crisis, I jump in to fix it.* Beth realizes that her pattern is not only reinforcing but also encouraging Ali's pattern of behavior.

We are not our children, and we don't imprint them as a mirror of ourselves. Yet we do teach, often in unintended ways. We reinforce one another's patterns, sometimes across generations.

One day, when Max was about two years old, I was holding him as he fell asleep. I was reveling in the simple trust and love, the blissful perfection of holding my son. Listening to his breathing, I found my breath matching his, and his glowing toddler warmth turned me lethargic and contented.

I found myself entranced watching his tiny fingers. He went to sleep by rubbing a shred of his sheepskin fleece against his nose, and rolling the little piece of fuzz delicately over and over to comfort himself. Perhaps it was his rolling fingers that reminded me of my dad.

Growing Up with Patterns

My dad and mom divorced when I was just a year old. That day watching Max sleep, I remembered was how my dad used to tuck me in at night during my obligatory weekly visit. He'd lay down next to me for a few minutes and drum his fingers on the side of my bed.

When I was a kid, I thought the "finger drumming" was just a cool sound. I remember practicing it later, tapping each finger in a rapid cascade. My dad tucked me in because it was part of my mom's list of instructions. Given a man obsessed with his work and uncomfortable with children, the bedtime ritual was probably boring, or maybe just too intimate.

While this memory was painful, in the bliss of sleepy-Max I wasn't really upset. Instead I started to be curious. What did I learn from my dad's behavior? Do I follow some of the same patterns?

I think my dad found intimacy overwhelming, and the finger drumming was a way to distance himself. I already told you one of my patterns: When I feel overwhelmed, I withdraw.

I was also struck by our similarity in being obsessed with work. While I didn't drum my fingers in impatience when son was falling asleep, I certainly noticed that there were probably too many times when I was with him that I was thinking about work instead of giving him my full attention.

That day with Max, I wished that I would always be a dad who could hold his son in safe sheltering arms. A dozen years later, I'm sorry to report that there have been many days where I found myself in the same absent-father patterns. Yet there have been at least as many where I noticed what I was doing and chose to change my behavior.

THE OTHER LESSON

As I look at my own patterns, I see that sometimes my reactions are serving me well, and other times they are, well, not. One way to evaluate is to notice the "other lesson," the unintended collateral damage that comes with my unconscious reactions.

We're teaching our children every day. Some things we teach intentionally, and others are unintentional. We want our kid to clean up after himself. An intentional lesson is in the words we use: *Clean up your mess.* Then the unintentional one is in the way we deliver the words. Maybe it's with a bit of frustration and annoyance. Maybe then our child feels hurt hearing our tone of voice. The intentional lesson is the skill we want them to develop; the unintentional is how they end up feeling about this. The intentional lesson is what we mean for them to hear; the unintentional is what they actually take away.

We are constantly sending messages to the people around us, including our children. For some of those messages, we carefully think about the impact we want to have and chose our words, attitude, and timing. For example, if your shy child will soon attend preschool, most likely, you'll have some quiet, thought-out conversations about how she might cope in this new situation. This is an intentional lesson.

At the same time, we send unspoken messages. Our children observe our actions, they interpret our words, and they come to their own conclusions. If I want my daughter to be kind, and then scold her: *Be nice to your brother.* She hears the words, but the emotion is even louder, and she walks away thinking, *My brother sure causes me a lot of problems.* In addition to the lesson we mean to teach, there is another lesson constructed from nuance, emotion, and interpretation. This is what I call the "other lesson."

Other lessons are always present when we interact with others. There are moments when we deliver the other lesson with great effect – often accidentally! Years after I left the classroom, one of my students wrote

66

We send unspoken messages. Our children observe our actions, they interpret our words, and they come to their own conclusions.

99

me saying, "Do you remember when you said X, Y, or Z? I think about that all the time, and it's helped me become a better person." I had no recollection I'd said that.

Unintended Consequences

Sometimes the other lesson directly undermines the lesson we mean to teach as parents. All too often, and with the best of intentions, I'll attempt to "teach" my kids something, and the way I do it creates a terrible other lesson. I suspect that the times when I'm most serious about delivering intentional lessons are the times I'm most strongly delivering the other lessons.

One big challenge with the other lesson is you don't actually know what someone else is learning. They might not even realize it themselves. They might show you, or give you signals that help you guess. Some examples:

What I say	Possible other lesson
Be careful.	Don't be independent.
Let me explain how to do this.	I don't trust you.
Settle down and do your work.	Work is a negative experience.

One of the absolute essentials for living and leading with EQ is being mindful of these emotional exchanges. What emotional messages am I sending? What lesson am I really teaching?

One day I was on an incessant string of phone calls from my home office. Max, now four years old, kept wandering by. At some point, I opened my door and he was standing waiting for me. He asked me a question that gave me a painful realization of the other lesson I'd been teaching him: "Are you in the mood for me now, Daddy?" In his question, I heard that I'd been teaching him that I don't like to be with him.

The lesson I wished he would learn from my work habits is about the importance of focus and perseverance. The other lesson he was internalizing is that I often don't want to be with him.

Fast-forward to the present day. I often think about the words of the Cat Stevens' song "Cat's in the Cradle" about the boy who wants his dad's attention, and when the dad finally "wakes up," the boy is too busy with his own life. My son is now at an age where he's increasingly independent. I want to spend time with him while he still wants to do things with me, but I'm still can't completely let go of my obsession with work.

I love my son, and I love my work. (How to find balance there is a whole other book, and there have already been hundreds, if not thousands, already written on it.) I have my patterns, Max has his, and together it's all too easy to slip into them. Yet if I am going to be the parent I want to be, then I have to fight this tendency. The first step is noticing my patterns, and looking for the other lesson is a way to help me pay attention.

Criticism and Praise

A related example: homework.

I want Max to take his work seriously and do his best. As a result, when I think he's being lazy, I criticize him. Many times that criticism escalates because of my fear, *What if he can't do well in school?* The fact that he has learning challenges increases my worries and fear, which makes me anxious. My pattern: When I'm afraid, I attack. So I raise my voice, and I'm stern, maybe even harsh.

The lesson I want to teach: *You can do better.*

The other lesson: *You are not good enough.*

The terrible irony: I learned this same other lesson from my own father. As a result, for years I doubted myself and underachieved. Writing this book has helped me clarify this dynamic, and I asked Max about it. His perspective surprised me. I knew that I was critical, but I thought I balanced criticism with praise.

Max's perspective: "Yes, you're critical, and yes, you praise me, but the criticism is clearer than the praise." Max told me that he doesn't really hear the praise because it's "just always there." I was trying to avoid the other lesson of my father's sparse praise and fell into a very different other lesson where praise became meaningless.

Such a complex balancing act! The only solution is to be mindful of these unfolding dynamics and to check in with yourself and your kids. Keep asking yourself: *What patterns am I following?* Keep noticing: *What are the lessons I mean to teach? What are the "other lessons" that I'm conveying?*

Part II covers tools and strategies to help change some pattern you'd like to change. But for now, the first step is to observe. The next chapter is about helping children increase their self-awareness, which also helps us as parents do the same.

What are the lessons I mean to teach?
What are the "other lessons" that I'm
conveying?

Chapter 3:

Helping Kids with Self-Awareness

While this book is about you as a parent, when I speak with parents about EQ, they also want to know: How do I teach these skills to my children? Here are a few ideas about helping your children become more self-aware.

First, some milestones, or goals, to consider what it might look like for a child to develop self-awareness.

Self-Awareness Goals

Ages 0–4: Identify big feelings – happy, sad, mad, afraid – and why you have these. Begin to notice that you have thoughts and feelings, and what you do when you have a big feeling.

Ages 5–7: Continue to name your feelings, expanding your vocabulary. Add the ideas that feeling can be more or less intense and feelings can motivate you. Recognize that your feelings push you to behave in certain ways. Learn the difference between thoughts, feelings, and actions and how to recognize examples in your own life.

Ages 8–11: Expand your vocabulary to describe feelings. Realize that basic emotions can combine into thousands of different emotions, all of which have different names. Learn that you have choices about feelings, thoughts, and actions and that they influence one another. Learn the concept of patterns and how to recognize and describe them: When (stimulus), I (typical reaction).

Ages 12–15: Learn the difference between similar feelings – such as distinguishing between frustration and anger. Learn that you can have multiple, layered feelings at the same time. Identify your frequently recurring patterns and be able to notice these reactions by yourself.

Ages 16+: Discover that feelings are a universal language, and speaking openly about feelings connects people. Come to see feelings as a source of insight and wisdom. Practice recognizing your patterns before anyone else notices – when the reaction is just getting started. Start to use emotions to understand inner self and interpersonal relationships.

ENHANCING EMOTIONAL LITERACY

In chapter one, we talked about *emotional literacy* being the ability to name and understand emotions. To help your child develop this skill, work to teach your child vocabulary to talk about emotions.

Emotion Coaching

A very effective way to develop emotional literacy is to talk to our children about feelings in a way that helps them give clear labels to their internal experiences. Emotions are very confusing, especially when they don't know how to name and talk about them. We can help them find words to accurately describe their internal experience. John Gottman, who is well known for his research about lasting marriages, calls this *emotion coaching*.

For example, when Emma was around three and Max around five, we went for a walk. It had been raining, and we arrived at the park to find it was covered with water. The play structure was like a bridge over a shallow lake.

We went home to see if our own sandbox was better. Since I believe it is validating for people to know that someone recognizes their feelings, I said, "Emma, this is disappointing, isn't it?" She agreed. Curious, I asked her what that word means.

"Sad, and angry," said Emma. Oh.

"Well, what about when Maxie has a toy you want, what is that?"

She said, "Angry, and also sad."

"What about when you want to do something, and I say *no*, what's that feeling?"

"That's sad, and angry," said Emma.

I laughed because she is so right: Most of these difficult situations feel a

Tools for Emotional Literacy

Try these techniques to help your child name and understand feelings:

Emotion coach. Make an observation and offer an emotion word to match. *I hear your voice is loud. Are you feeling angry?*

Emotion puzzles. Once a child is aware of some basic emotions, you can make a game of figuring out the ingredients in a feeling. *She seems jealous about her brother getting to use her toy. What emotions happen when someone feels jealous?*

Emotion stories. Part of emotional literacy is putting feelings into a logical sequence. *If Alexander is feeling mad and then he loses his lunch, what do you think he'll feel next?*

Tip: You can practice any of these tools with real-life situations and people, and/or when reading a story or watching a show.

lot alike. There are subtle blends of anger, sorrow, and fear that signal us about problems.

We continued to discuss all the different words to describe emotions that I could think of. I suggested that when Max has a toy she wants, that might also be called jealousy. She said jealousy is also when you are really angry, and sad, because you don't get to have the toy.

Here are some of the other examples we discussed:

> Frustration is when you want Daddy to bring your drink right now, but he takes a long time.

> Remorse is when you do something you wish you had not done.

> Rage is when you are so mad you want to bite or hit.

> Joy is when you are so happy and excited you jump instead of walk.

Of course, there are many other emotions and words to describe them. Over the years, we talked more about fear, sorrow, grief, acceptance, and other feelings that create the richness of life.

When you are coaching your child about emotions, remember your job is to observe – not to direct. State what you notice and offer a suggestion or ask a question. For example: "I hear your voice is raised. Is that because you are angry? Or are you scared?"

TEACHING CHILDREN ABOUT PATTERNS

Once you begin to understand patterns and the way emotions drive your own "autopilot" reactions, it's time to help your children begin to see theirs. For some reason, even though I've worked with thousands of professionals to do this, it was eluding me in my own home.

This came clearly into focus for me when Emma's four-and-a-half-year-old priorities conflicted with Max's two-and-a-half-year-old priorities. Add two workaholic parents and their own stresses, and voila, you have a powder keg. It got to the point I was looking forward to traveling, so I could have a few days of peace. I took that as a bad sign.

Around this time, I met with Karen McCown, Six Seconds' chairman and founder. We talked frequently about my little family and about her grandchildren. As many blog readers have told me, grandparent-hood sounds like the best of parenting: all the love, none of the "hot buttons."

The day after my chat with Karen, I happened to be at a party with some colleagues, and we were at a table with some random strangers, one of whom was a psychotherapist. I talked to my friends about my struggles at home, and the therapist chimed in. I was struck by the dramatic difference between the therapist's approach and Karen's.

The therapist said, "It sounds like you are letting you kids run things in your house, and you can't do that."

Somewhat testy, I said, "Actually, I *can* do it, but I agree it might not be a good idea."

"You need to be clear about who's in charge," she went on, ignoring my jibe, "and consistently reward the appropriate behavior and have consequences for the inappropriate behavior. You have to be more consistent."

Not terrible advice for a cocktail party. Then I considered Karen's advice from the evening before and how different it was.

Starting With Patterns

First Karen asked me what is happening: *What's the pattern?* I explained that a conflict escalated, Emma's behavior got explosive, and I sent her to time-out or her room.

"Is that working?" asked Karen.

"Not really."

"So you probably don't want to keep doing it, do you?" I shook my head. "Do you and Emma talk about what happened?"

"Emma would rather not," I said, starting to feel a bit pathetic. How did I give a four-and-a-half-year-old so much power?

After a few more minutes, Karen summarized our discussion into this experiment: "Why don't you try this: Next time you send Emma to her room, say, 'When you are ready to talk about what happened, come get me.' Then discuss what happened and make an agreement about what Emma and you will do differently next time. Write it down where Emma can see it."

Therapy vs. EQ

Before I tell you what happened, let's look at the difference between Karen's advice and the therapist's. Notice who had the power or "right" in the adult-to-adult conversations. The therapist told me what I "had" to do. Karen asked me what was important for me to do. The therapist told me the answer; she "knew better." Karen asked me questions, giving me a message that I could figure this out.

Also notice how each approach changes the power dynamic between Emma and me. One actually escalates the power struggle; the other sidesteps it. The therapist focused on the behavior, my daughter's and mine. Karen focused on what was under the behavior. The therapist told me I needed to take charge and use my power as a parent over Emma. Karen emphasized the power of alignment and working together to solve Emma and my shared problem.

Tools for Recognize Patterns

Try these techniques to assist children to notice their frequently recurring reactions.

Pattern detective. We constantly follow patterns. Make it a game to recognize them.

How's that working? Once you recognize a pattern, ask yourself or your child the classic EQ question: *How is that working for you?* More specifically: *Is this working out the way you wanted it to?* These questions are actually about consequential thinking (explained in Part II), but they can help us clarify patterns too.

When you're ready. There's no need to talk about an incident immediately after it happens. Sometimes we need to de-escalate and reflect. That's the original intention of a time-out. When you and your child are both ready, talk.

Karen used the *Self-Science* process. Self-Science is a method for teaching about emotions. Karen described it in the book *Self-Science: The Emotional Intelligence Curriculum*, originally published in 1978 and now in its third edition.

Self-Science is a process for teaching people to make more conscious choices. It begins by taking inventory: noticing thoughts, feelings, and actions and then identifying patterns – to observe yourself like a scientist. This is the same concept as Know Yourself, the first step in the Six Seconds Model (see page 19), and is what I've been talking about in the book up to now.

The next step is to evaluate, and then to consciously choose – this is the focus of Part II, Choose Yourself, the second step in the Six Seconds Model. Self-Science works in a cycle: Once you choose, you can go back and observe again.

My sense is that Karen's advice also focused on the long term vs. the short term. Emma needs to make decisions for herself, and eventually these will be fairly serious decisions. What am I doing now to equip her for that challenge? I'll talk more about this in Part III, Give Yourself, the third step in the Six Seconds Model.

When You Are Ready to Talk

A few days after talking to Karen and the therapist, one of the "inevitable" conflicts between Emma and me occurred. I had a surprising experience. While I was caught up in the conflict, I did not feel the need to explode. I didn't feel hopeless. This is the power of having a new strategy.

I asked Emma if she wanted to talk about what happened. As usual, she grouched, "No!" I followed Karen's advice and said: "That's fine. When you're ready to talk about it, come get me." Just a few minutes later, Emma did just that. I began my Self-Science process and asked, "What happened?"

Emma had trouble telling the story, and I realized that looking at the whole event was too complex at her age. Instead, I began telling her what I thought had happened. After each little piece, I asked if she agreed – really asked, not to push her to agree with me, but to get her view. We agreed on some parts, not others, and didn't debate it – we each saw the story from our own side.

Then I identified the part that was upsetting for me: "I felt ignored when I told you to stop grabbing your brother for the second time and it did not seem like you listened. Were you listening?"

"No," said Emma. I could see the realization sink in.

I told Emma that I wanted to write down what she would do differently and what I would do differently next time. I taped a sheet of paper to her closet door (easily visible) and I asked what I should write. Emma said, "No Ignoring."

We All Need Strategies

I was surprised again when the next day there was a minor tussle between Emma and Max. When I asked what happened, Emma told me. After identifying the issue, *Emma* said we needed to write a new note on the closet door.

I suspect that a large part of my own reactivity with the kids came from feeling powerless – like this won't end, and I can't stop it. Probably Emma was experiencing much the same thing. Karen's suggestion gave me the comfort of having a new strategy, and I think it did the same for Emma.

The takeaways for me were:

- Keep practicing optimism. A conflict won't last forever, and I can choose to act differently.

- Keep experimenting with new ways of communicating.

- Stay away from power struggles. Make my job "help them learn" rather than "enforce."

- Help my children discover their own patterns of behavior – the process is sincerely asking questions, rather than "giving advice."

- Stay engaged. Talk. Not in the moment of conflict, but soon after.

My other realization is about the intersection of my patterns and Emma's. As you can see in the story, one of Emma's patterns was, "When I feel angry, I don't talk."

There are two patterns that are frequent challenges for me. My "dragon patterns" that can fuel an epic internal battle are:

- When I feel powerless, I attack.

- When I feel overwhelmed, I withdraw.

Can you see how Emma's and my patterns are at odds in a conflict? As my child moves into a power struggle and I don't know what to do, I quickly escalate. Then I want to run away.

As conflicts intensified, both of our patterns were conspiring to shut down communication. It was easier for me to let her not talk, because this helped me follow my pattern. She could slam her door, I could slam mine, and we could both feel righteous.

I suspect this will be true of your patterns as well. When you identify one of yours, does it reinforce one of your child's patterns? Does your child's pattern reinforce one of yours?

DISCIPLINE STRATEGIES

Of course, the most problematic patterns emerge when we're the most frustrated with our children's behavior or feel helpless to change it. I like the concept of positive discipline and using natural consequences, instead of punishment. But when you've told your kid four times to get off Minecraft and do his homework and he's still pretending he can't hear you, it can feel like these techniques just aren't going to cut it.

When it comes to figuring out what approach to discipline works for your family, think about the one piece of advice I gave in the preface of this book: Make it a learning process. So experiment keeping these points in mind:

1. Pick your battles.

Yes, it's a cliché, but still so important in dealing with your kids. You can fight with your kids about bedtime, or homework, or screen time, or manners, or chores.... The list never ends, so don't take them on all at once. If you're fighting on too many fronts, most likely your child will end up overwhelmed and you'll end up frustrated. When you take one issue on, do it for real and make it one that really matters to you.

2. You don't need to decide on the spot.

Of the million challenges you face a week as a parent, almost none actually require a decision in that instant. Give *yourself* a time-out, and then decide how to respond after you've calmed down. It doesn't even need to be the same day. When you do this, you're able to think more clearly about your reaction. Also by telling your child, "I need to think about this," you're modeling coping behavior that includes taking the time to react thoughtfully.

3. You have many, many options.

When we feel frustrated, it's hard to be creative, and that can lead us to feel helpless, as if there are scant options. Time-out on the couch, floor, steps, next to me, far from me, with your bear, with your book. Talking about what happened, writing about what happened. Adding chores, taking away privileges. No one approach will work perfectly or all the time. Yes, consistency is good, but so is flexibility. Experiment to find what works, with what kid, under what circumstances.

One caution: remember the "other lesson," which accompanies every intentional lesson. Don't accidentally teach that your love is conditional, that you don't trust your child, or that your child can't trust you.

Why Behavior Problems Occur

We all have triggers – things that push our patterns into motion. They might be hot buttons that make us want to explode or cold buttons that make us want to shut down.

As you work to use emotional intelligence to foster positive, collaborative behavior, consider that "bad behavior" comes for a reason. Get curious about it. Ask: *What's driving this behavior?* Remember that emotions are fuel pushing the patterns forward – patterns connected to fear or anger or hurt are usually a form of self-protection. The bigger those feelings, the more powerfully we get locked into the patterns.

There are some triggers that frequently elicit problematic behavior. For example, parents and children are likely to be more reactive when they are hungry, angry, lonely, or tired (HALT). When you notice tension building, think "HALT" as a reminder to slow down and consider if one of these factors is at play.

Another avenue to explore: Emotions are contagious, so it's no surprise that your children will often mirror your mood and vice versa. Have you noticed that when you are tired and stressed, often your children are tired and stressed around the same time? When you get into power struggle, they are probably also in power struggle. When you are sad, they might also feel sad. When you feel stuck, they probably do too.

So when you're trying to understand why your child is reacting, consider your own feelings. When stress and frustration rise, give yourself a break, give your kid a break, and then come back to the table and learn together.

Tools for Discipline

Practice these ideas to create positive, collaborative behavior:

Step by step. Parenting is a marathon, not a sprint. Pick one challenge and work on it. Then choose another. Then come back and do the first again. (Yes, you will need to tell them a million times; it's part of the challenge.)

More options. Remember you have a lot of options for discipline. Don't get stuck playing the same note over and over. Google is your friend; there are a million ideas out there. None will work perfectly. Experiment and adapt to find what works for your family.

HALT checklist. When you or your children are reactive, stop and notice if you or they are hungry, angry, lonely, or tired. Address those needs, rather than letting these common triggers kick off negative patterns of behavior.

THE UGLY SECRETS OF PARENTHOOD: WRAPPING UP PART I

Yes, parenting is the most difficult job I can imagine. No, I don't feel qualified. Many days I wonder how it can possibly work out. And yet even in the midst of ugliness, there's something magical about being "Daddy." When I'm distressed, I remember there have been worse days,

Perhaps our most unglamorous day parenting began around ten years ago just before Christmas. Right at 7 a.m., Emma bounded into our room excited about getting ready for the "annual" holiday tea later in the day ("annual" meaning we'd done this the year before, so of course we had to do it again).

First, Emma decided she wanted to wear the same dress she wore last year. Patty had purchased a new holiday dress and thought it was reasonable that the Emma wear the new dress to tea. Emma had other plans. It seems the biggest fights occur about the smallest issues.

We thought it was a reasonable request. Emma did not. This fight continued for six hours, escalating gradually into a scene I would prefer to forget. After dozens of strategies and attempts, we all but forced Emma into the new blue dress. She made her displeasure known.

The dress conflict culminated in, "Damn it, Emma, fine, you do whatever you want. Just get out of our room and leave us alone for awhile," followed by a half hour of her sobbing. Patty said, "Great, we've spent the day teaching our daughter that if she whines and cries, she gets what she wants. And that we are mean about it."

Somehow the tempest finally settled, and it was time to leave. I'd love to say the heavens opened with light, but actually it started to pour buckets of rain. We struggled through the deluge into the car.

The Tea Party

Instead of being in the glorious hotel ballroom, the holiday tea party was in a thoroughly beige, little boxy meeting room with low ceilings. Things looked up when "Sphinkie the Elf" came out to sing and dance with a six-foot bear. Yes, parenthood will reduce you to toe tapping and singing along with a goofy elf.

Emma and her friend had a delightful time and acted like angels. It seemed that the day was turning around. We drove back through the storm, stopped to pick up Chinese food, and put the kids to bed.

After this kind of day, we needed a break, and sat back to watch a movie. Prophetically, it was *The Divine Secrets of the Ya-Ya Sisterhood*. There's a scene in the middle where the mom is falling apart trying to deal with four vomiting children. Watching that, my stomach was starting to roil. "Wow, that looks horrible," I thought. "I'm glad it's not me." Do you hear the foreshadowing?

Candles and Romance

Yes. Right before bed, Patty and I both got sick to our stomachs. We had eaten something wonky. We both figured it was probably the $200 tea – just a little cosmic joke. Suffice it to say, neither of us could sleep, and every hour one of us would bolt for the toilet.

Then the power went out. It was a *big* rainstorm.

My next trip to the bathroom included a splash in the dark as I walked across a sodden corner of the carpet. The flooding had begun. I am Not Kidding. There was good inch and a half of water on our bedroom floor.

Trying to get warm back in bed, I said to Patty, "At least Emma seems ok." Ten minutes later, Emma arrives in our room crying. We both get up. Patty hands me our "third child," Buddy Bear, who is covered in vomit. As I go to clean him, I start throwing up again. Patty takes Emma (and the flashlight) away and leaves me kneeling in the dark.

A few minutes later, Patty comes back with a lighted taper. Who says parenting is not romantic? Vomit by candlelight – very picturesque.

We put Emma back to bed, and Max woke up excited to see the candles. He had managed to pee out the side of his diaper. Two changed beds, two sets of changed jammies, and a couple more stops by the toilet for each of us, and everyone was back to bed.

The Secret

The power returned just before dawn, and the lights came blinking back on waking me up. Finally, I found my way back to bed, cold, aching, feverish, and soggy.

These are secrets they never tell to people before parenthood lest the species die out. As long as I am breaking the silence, though, there is one more secret you have to know:

At 3:30 a.m., Patty was tucking Max in, and I was tucking Emma in. I pulled two blankets up around her because of the cold and touched her face. Emma looked at me, smiled, and said, "I love you, Daddy Bear." The awfulness of this endless night evaporated.

It is astounding how love changes your perspective. The next morning, 24 hours after the dress-fight started, Emma and I were lying on the couch, her head on my arm. As the sun came up, I didn't care that the water damage repair was going on the credit card; it didn't matter that my stomach felt like a football team had been practicing on me. Because I had something more elusive, more lasting, and more powerful.

This strange paradox is driving me, and I suspect it's driving you, too, to be a better parent tomorrow.

It is astounding how love changes your perspective.

PART II

Choose Yourself

*How can we do more of what
we actually mean to do?*

In Part II:

Introduction: Choosing to Choose Myself

Chapter 4: From Reaction to Response

> **Apply consequential thinking**: Pause and look ahead to see if you're creating the results you want.
>
> **Navigate emotions**: Use emotions to move forward in a positive way.

Chapter 5: Creating New Possibilities

> **Engage intrinsic motivation**: Tap into drivers such as safety, belonging, achievement, and purpose to create powerful commitment.
>
> **Exercise optimism**: Create new options to solve your challenges.

Chapter 6: Helping Children Choose Themselves

INTRODUCTION:

Choosing to Choose Myself

In Part I, we got to know ourselves – and maybe you're seeing some patterns that are highly functional and some that are less functional. Maybe you identified a pattern "When I feel challenged, I listen more carefully" – and it's helping you connect with your children. Or maybe you've recognized a pattern "When I feel hurt, I hurt others" – and you're thinking: *I don't want to teach this one to my kids.*

Just because you have a pattern, you don't have to continue to follow it. We don't have to keep being the person or parent we were yesterday, and we all can learn something new or decide to change the way we act.

When Max was born, I suddenly faced a whole new level of fear about myself as a father. Would I abandon him? Would I push him away? Would I make him feel inadequate, and even unworthy of love? In short, *Would I be like my dad?*

My friends and colleagues, especially those who knew my dad, scoffed at this. "You're nothing like him," was the common response. Yet I know this to be untrue. I am very much like him. I have many of his mannerisms, I look like him, and I repeat many of his patterns. I shared this one already: "When I feel overwhelmed, I withdraw." He was very good at withdrawing.

These reassurances failed, and I was afraid of myself.

When Max was about two years old, I was in Mexico working with a remarkable educator named Angelica Malpica. She and her husband owned and ran a school for over 2,500 students, and she was interested in emotional intelligence. She taught classes to parents about tuning into their own emotions. The classes were free, but if you joined, you were committed to attending all eight (or so) over a series of Saturdays. At that point, she had four different classes going, each with 500 parents enrolled.

A tiny Mexican woman, she'd stand on a makeshift stage in basement room of the school with 500 parents, and she'd command the whole room. Fiery, vibrant, passionate – those were words made for Angelica. And she saw inside people.

We were eating tacos and drinking Corona in a little restaurant, and in English and broken Spanish I told her of my fear that I would be distant with Max like my dad had been with me.

"This is your father," Angelica said, placing a beer bottle. "And this is your son," placing another bottle two hand-spans away from the first. "Here you are" (placing a third bottle in between, which she then turns 180°), "but you are facing your father. You need to go to him and forgive him, so that you can turn and face your son." At that point, I didn't actually want to forgive my dad, but I asked her what she meant. A decade later, I still hear her voice:

"You must go to your father and bow down and tell him: 'I am grateful for the gift of my life. Your future is not my destiny.'"

I don't know if it was the broken language, or the beer, or the Mexican magical realism, but this was not adding up for me. I explained that I was *always* the one who went to him, that I did *all* the work in the "relationship," such as it was. "That is the order of nature," Angelica said. "The son goes to the father."

Hmmmm. This was just too much. I could not even begin to imagine telling him, "Your future is not my destiny," and I was totally fed up with his unwillingness, or inability, to pick up the phone once or twice a year.

Still something about that conversation kept rattling around in my head. And my fear wasn't going away. I decided to do some experiments with Angela's advice.

My first experiment was to see if, in the privacy of my own thoughts, I could tell my dad, "I love you." Just that, "I love you" without the "*but* how could you abandon us?" It seems almost silly to me now, but I could not do it, even in my own head. I did love him, I did feel some gratitude, and at the same time: I blamed and judged him.

Making Others Good

Again, I went to Six Seconds' founder Karen McCown for her advice. To summarize several conversations, she asked me to consider a powerful question:

If I had his skills and experiences, could I have done any better?

I began to see that his bad parenting was the product of *his* life experience – not mine. He didn't do a good job, but maybe he did as well as he could?

One of the lessons Karen has shared with our team is that the way we think about others matters: We can make others bad, or we can make them good. Making somebody bad is easy. We tell ourselves other people are stupid, wrong, ignorant, incompetent, or evil, and they dress like dorks. Consider these scenarios:

> In line waiting for the agent to check your family into a flight and thinking: *Come ON, how hard can it be?*

> Looking at a child's misbehavior and saying to your partner: *That's* your *son/daughter.*

> Gossiping with a friend: *Can you believe she lets her kids be on the computer as much as they want?*

In part, we make others bad because it feels good. It can give us a sense of superiority. We feel righteous. In fact, our brains give us a dopamine reward when we are certain, when we are right, and when we know better. (Dopamine is a heroin-like neurohormone, a little treat our brain gives itself to reinforce certain responses.)

The alternative is to make people good. It's just a different way of thinking. For example, we can tell ourselves: *He's doing the best he can, and I could do no better.* (Note: Don't make yourself bad either – it's not about one over the other.) To make someone good, you hold that person as equally dignified, smart, and skilled as you see yourself. In a religious context, this phrase reflects this same concept: "We are all children of God." Making others good is about fundamentally respecting people as equal. Easy to say. Hard to put into action consistently. Personally, I find it a lot easier with strangers.

When I began to practice thinking about my dad this way, my attitude began to shift. He did the best he could given his skills and experience. If I had his life – his abusive mother, wheelchair-bound father, obsessive gift with mathematics – I couldn't have done any better.

It took months, maybe even years, of occasionally practicing this new way of thinking. Eventually, though, something shifted inside me. From this shift, three surprising things happened:

1. I began to appreciate my father more, and to appreciate things in myself that I see coming from him. My grandmother often says, "Oh, you look just like your father." It used to offend me, even outrage me. One time this happened in the midst of my Angelica-inspired experiments, and suddenly it did not bother me. Now it even makes me proud.

2. I became less afraid of my relationship with my son, Max, and I let myself be more honest and more deeply connected with him.

3. My dad suddenly called me – for the first time in my adult life, he asked me to come see him.

After his call, I immediately knew something was wrong. I drove up the next day. In the course of about two minutes, he said, "Come on in. Have a cup of tea. I'm dying of cancer."

He was in his late sixties then and seemed quite fit, so it was surprising. But perhaps more surprising was this comment: "I wanted to tell you because of our relationship." He didn't actually want to tell anyone but his wife, but he chose to tell me. I was touched. Somehow as I changed my thinking and feeling about him, it changed our relationship.

Just to be clear: I did not say anything to him about Angela's beer-bottle advice or this whole "making him good" process. I didn't tell him I loved him – I was way too scared to do that. Yet when I started making him good, just inside my own head, something changed between us.

This is a big deal, and I've seen it over and over in my life. It's a central idea in the Six Seconds Model of emotional intelligence. We don't get to control others – we can't even completely control ourselves. But when we Choose Ourselves, when we take full ownership of *our* end of the relationship, the relationship changes too.

How Do We Get People to Change?

This has a profound implication for us as parents. I mean, we love our kids, and we all want them to learn, to get better, to stretch. That means we want them to change – the kind of positive change that's at the core of Six Seconds' purpose. We want them to be kind, motivated, and brilliant...good at sports, school, friendships...and to pick up their toys, clean their rooms without being asked, and stop arguing with their siblings. This list is endless.

How do we foster these changes?

The conventional approach is to try to get kids to change through incentives or punishments – carrots and sticks. "If you pick up your toys, we'll have ice cream." "If you don't pick up your train set, I'll take it away for a week." This sort of works, at least in the short term. But as I'll explain in Chapter 5, the more we focus on these external tools, the less our children will be internally motivated (also called *intrinsically* motivated), an ability they need to be able to achieve on their own.

What do we do instead? This might be a difficult pill to swallow, but the answer is: If we want our kids to change, we need to change.

Think about the "other lesson" (page 55), where we accidentally teach our kids to internalize something destructive. We can change that lesson by changing our reactions. As we get off autopilot, step away from power struggles, and move away from making others bad, we're able to build trustworthy relationships with our kids. We can have open, honest dialogue and enjoy mutual respect. From there, we can focus not just on the surface behavior, but also on the deeper drivers of our own and our kids' choices.

No, it's not easy, and it's not a one-off. We don't just flip a switch and stay in a positive parenting relationship. It's a long, continuous process. We have to keep Choosing Ourselves over and over – and as we do that we create an opportunity for our children to do the same.

So how do we actually do this? In the EQ model, we've defined four skills needed to be able to Choose Ourselves, which I'll explain in the next chapters.

> **"**
>
> As we get off autopilot, step away from power struggles, and move away from making others bad, we're able to build trustworthy relationships with our kids.
>
> **"**

Chapter 4:

From Reaction to Response

In Part I, we looked at the automatic patterns that we've learned to follow. Often those patterns are a reaction to a stressor. I told the story of how two-year-old-Emma hit me in the nose, and I almost hit her back: I was reacting.

In *Man's Search for Meaning*, Viktor Frankl wrote:

> *Between stimulus and response there is a space. In that space is our power to choose our response. In our response lies our growth and our freedom.*

Now that we know that the space is there (and from Part I you know it's about a half second), how do we utilize it? Key to moving from reaction to response is practicing the first two competencies in Choosing Yourself: apply consequential thinking and navigate emotions.

Apply Consequential Thinking

Max, my son, was fairly impulsive when he was two years old (and considerably less so now he's 14). Maybe "spontaneous and carefree" would be a rosier description. I can't even begin to count how many times Patty or I have said, "Think before you start." For example, one day when he was 11, on the very busy streets of Bangkok, Max practically jumped off the curb into the path of an oncoming motorcycle –

> "
>
> If you go down this path, how will it
> work out? How will you and others
> feel? Now? Later? It's a balancing of
> self and other, now and later, want
> and need.
>
> "

illustrating an ongoing lack of "applying consequential thinking." On the other hand, Max sometimes now starts to speak then pauses and says, "Never mind. If I said it, things wouldn't go well for me." Small triumph!

That small pause to evaluate requires many brain areas to work together. When Max pauses, he has a feeling, probably triggered from his *basal ganglia*, the part of the brain that gives messages about what to do and what not to do. He blends that with input from his *prefrontal cortex*, the "executive function" area of the brain that helps him evaluate (problematically, this is most likely the last part of the brain to fully develop, taking as much as 24 years before it reaches optimal structure). In under a quarter of a second, those messages integrate with signals from his emotional, motor, and sensory areas, all balancing together to allow him to pause and assess.

Applying consequential thinking, or ACT, is a little like strategic planning but with a big focus on emotion. If you go down this path, how will it work out? How will you and others feel? Now? Later? It's a balancing of self and other, now and later, want and need. There are many confounding factors that make this extremely difficult.

Here are three:

1. Stress, in general, is a signal of potential danger. It puts our brain and body on alert, making us more reactive – more likely to follow survival-oriented patterns stored in an area of the brain called the *amygdala*. The amygdala focuses on self-preservation. It reacts when we perceive that we're under threat and causes the urgent and self-interested reactions: fight, flee, or freeze. As stress increases, just as our heartbeat accelerates, so does our decision-making speed. In order to increase speed, our brain tosses nuance overboard. Decisions become less careful, less balanced, and shorter term.

For instance, if I'm arguing with Max and my stress rises (hard to imagine), my amygdala will become very active, pressuring me to protect myself. That stress tells my brain: *Danger! You better fight!* In response, I'm predisposed to follow patterns of attacking or defending.

In my case, my fallback pattern in this situation is to fight, to escalate by using the power of my position: "If you don't finish your homework right now, no computer time for a week."

2. Task orientation, like stress, involves a narrowing of attention. Remember that applying consequential thinking requires integrating a range of data: Task focus is about ignoring everything but the task. It's a powerful skill that helps us be successful at accomplishing a lot of work; the tradeoff is we ignore everything else.

Imagine Max comes home feeling sad about something, and I'm trying to finish a chapter of a book. If I'm fighting with myself to stay focused on my task, chances are I will completely miss any nuance of the "Hey" when he comes in that could tip me off that something is amiss. (I've most likely been procrastinating off and on all day, so add stress to this story too.)

In other words, the harder we're working to get a task completed, the less bandwidth we have to pay attention to emotional data, such as our child's tone of voice or body language.

3. Suppression allows us to ignore our own emotional warning signals. An extreme case is a soldier walking into a hostile situation and having to suppress very strong emotional signals that say, "Do Not Take Another Step!" Suppression greatly helps in certain parenting situations too. It allows us to do things that make us uncomfortable, such as talking to our child about sex, and to take risks, such as snowboarding with our kids (I tried that... once).

Suppression can backfire though. For example, starting when she was young, Emma often felt anxious. Sometimes she would work so hard to ignore and push away the anxiety that she'd actually make herself feel ill (then she'd feel anxious about feeling sick). When we overuse suppression, the price can be huge. Emotions provide essential feedback about our relationships and ourselves. When we get "too good" at suppressing feelings, we can't tell when we're hurting others or ourselves.

Assess Yourself

Stress, task orientation, and suppression make it harder to be able to apply consequential thinking. Try thinking about how each of these three factors affects you on a scale of 1 to 5:

I am under significant, frequent stress.
1=Not at all true............... 5=Absolutely.

I am good at focusing on tasks.
1=Nope.................. 5=Sorry, what? I was doing something else.

I can ignore discomfort to do something important.
1=No risks for me............ 5=BRING IT!

By the way, stress, task orientation, and suppression also tend to be wrapped up in our patterns. If you are scoring yourself on toward the "5" end of these scales, you might also consider how these trigger your patterns, or how these result from your patterns.

In our research, men are generally weaker at ACT than women. In fact, of all the EQ competencies, it's the one where women have the biggest lead. I suspect that one reason is that men are socialized to engage in stress, focus on tasks (rather than people), and push aside discomfort to persevere. This brings my high-school coach vividly to mind. "*Come on,* girls" was the least offensive of his reminders that we "men" were supposed to be tough. The challenge is to be tough *and* smart, and that requires accessing the data that emotions can provide.

ACT does not mean being driven by emotion. Quite the contrary. It means being thoughtful. Evaluative. Balanced. Careful. Exercising mature judgment. Nor does it mean being boring: If you're good at applying consequential thinking, you know when to take risks, like letting your child climb that rock in the park – while keeping a close eye on him. ACT helps you know when to push past discomfort vs. the times when your discomfort is a message that needs attention, like that moment when you think, "It's a little *too* quiet in this house." ACT helps you put on the brakes, but it also helps you know when to be spontaneous. On the other hand, if you're not good at applying consequential thinking, your behavior might be likened to a bull in a china shop.

66

The challenge is to be tough *and* smart, and that requires accessing the data that emotions can provide.

99

THE THREE PROBLEM Ps

Applying consequential thinking to parenting requires us to integrate short-term and long-term thinking. We need to pay attention to the current situation and lesson to be learned, as well as "the other lesson" that our child will internalize over time (see page 55).

Recently, I observed a mom scolding a teacher. The mom was picking up her 10-year-old. Apparently he wore his coat all day. Mom: "What! He must have been so hot. Why didn't you take his coat off?" On one hand, the mom wants to protect her child and make sure he's comfortable. On the other, by expecting the teacher to make decisions about his clothing, she's teaching her son to be helpless. If this mom were to apply consequential thinking, she might say: *If he feels too uncomfortable, he'll take off his coat on his own.*

It's tough to see our children struggle – yet they need to struggle to learn, grow, and become independent. With enough ACT, we can evaluate and decide how much challenge is appropriate. There's no universal rule, the point is that we need to evaluate each situation mindfully rather than reacting on autopilot. If we could use this skill, it might alleviate these three problematic "P" parenting trends:

Passive: I often notice parents ignoring or excusing their child's misbehavior. Maybe they'll call across the room for Joey to stop taking toys, but they don't get up and intervene. *Parenting is an active sport.*

Perfectionist: I see parents, especially in affluent areas, who are terrified that their child will somehow be damaged by anything, no matter how trivial, that impinges on their idea of a perfect childhood. For example, if everything doesn't go exactly as planned at their child's birthday party, they treat it as a crisis rather than laughing about it and moving on. *Parenting is a long game.*

Protective (over!): I see parents who try so hard to protect their children that they undermine their growth. For example, I observed a child at a school who was talking trash, undermining the teacher, and, when asked, making excuses. The teacher told me she felt powerless to do anything, because the parent complains so vehemently whenever she tries to correct the child. Just as the child is full of excuses, so is the parent: "He just didn't hear you." Or, "He thought that word meant something else." *Parenting is letting children grow.*

This issue of overprotection and helicopter parenting has become pervasive. I'll give three more examples:

1. A few years ago, I talked to a mom in a very affluent area. She told me, "When the kids are home by themselves, they have to lock the door and turn on the alarm." Her kids were 12 and 14. Yes, our children are precious and life is risky, but do we really want to teach them to hide away? Are we making them more fragile by overprotecting them? What is the other lesson they're learning from the mom's fear?

2. Journalist Lenore Skenazy was dubbed "America's Worst Mom." She wrote an opinion piece in the *New York Sun* about letting her son ride the subway home by himself. She was deluged by "You're a terrible parent" emails. She did some research and then wrote the book *Free Range Kids*. She found that despite the hype, there has been no real increase in crimes against children, and your child is 32 times as likely to be hurt in his own car in his car seat then to be the victim of a crime against children. Yet in the United States today, many parents are extremely anxious about letting their children do activities that were normal for many of us growing up, like riding a bike to the grocery store, or playing with a random mix of neighborhood kids on the street. Of course, I want my kids to be safe. I also want them to live their lives as active, engaged people who take risks, learn, and participate in the world.

3. At around age nine, Emma was in a chorus audition. Afterward, we asked, "How did you do?" "I don't know," Emma said. We thought the teachers must have said something and asked her. "Yes," she said, "but adults always say you did well, even if you didn't, so I couldn't tell." If this is a widespread experience, then perhaps in protecting children from "low self-esteem," we've become so praising that it's meaningless.

The common theme in the problematic Ps is a lack of consequential thinking. Parents struggling with these are not bad people; they are not ill intentioned. They just are not connecting the dots to see how their choices are undermining their children. As we apply consequential thinking to parenting, we can move away from automatic reactions and become more careful and intentional in our responses.

The solution: Apply consequential thinking. Pause for a moment (or for six seconds) and look ahead.

THE SIX SECOND PAUSE

Remember that the chemicals of emotions last for about six seconds? When we're reacting, pausing for six seconds can make a tremendous difference.

There's a little part of the brain called the *thalamus*. It's a kind of regulator for sensory input, and one of its jobs is to watch for stress and threat. Depending on your stress level, it will route signals differently. When we're relaxed, our various brain areas work well together. For example, you're happily playing in the sandbox at the park with your child. The thalamus sends signals back and forth between our emotional and rational brain areas. That makes it possible to apply consequential thinking.

Under threat, or even the perception of threat, the thalamus has a different reaction. For example, another child comes up and you think he's threatening your child. Because of that perceived threat, the thalamus bypasses the cortex – the thinking brain – and sends the signal straight to the amygdala (the brain's fight-flight-freeze reaction center).

Sometimes this kind of reaction can save our lives. More frequently, it leads us to say something harmful, to escalate the situation, or even to act violently. For example, if you start yelling at that child you've perceived as a threat, you are escalating the situation. Especially if that child's parent then yells back. Soon there's war instead of collaboration. As neuroscientist Joseph LeDoux described it, in this interaction: Your amygdala is hijacking your brain.

Yes, your brain and body are flooded with emotion-chemicals pushing you to react — to fight, flee, or freeze.

You do not need to stay in that hijacked state. Yes, your brain and body are flooded with emotion-chemicals pushing you to react – to fight, flee, or freeze. But you still have choices, for example, picking up your crying child, moving out of the sandbox, and empathizing with your child – and even with the other child and parent.

The remedy is to slow down and practice patterns that do not escalate. It turns out that in about six seconds, the *cortex* (the logical part of the brain) can catch up with the *limbic* brain (the emotional reaction center). As a result of that pause and shift to get both parts of the brain working together, you are able to create a conscious, thoughtful response.

An emotional intelligence tool, which we aptly call the *Six Second Pause*, capitalizes on this process. It's a very simple, effective way to slow down and get your brain back in balance when your amygdala takes over. The goal is give yourself time to evaluate your options and decide what you want to do next.

To use a Six Second Pause, simply focus on listing six things that require an effort from you to think about. When you spend six seconds engaged in something that requires higher-order thinking (such as math or a foreign language) it slows your reaction and lets the different parts of your brain come back toward equilibrium. But it can't be too easy! You really need to think (that's why counting to 10 doesn't work).

Here are some examples of a Six Second Pause:

- Name six songs you like all with the letter "B" in the title.

- Identify six places you want to travel in alphabetical order.

- List six of your favorite movie characters and the films they were in.

- Think of six places you'd like to go on a family vacation.

- Your turn!

Once your pause button becomes "too easy" create a new one to keep your cognitive brain engaged.

Practicing ACT

Once you've taken that Six Second Pause, how do you apply consequential thinking? Ask yourself evaluative questions, for example:

- What are the pros and cons?

- What might happen next?

- What is the other lesson I'm teaching?

Ask yourself feeling questions too:

- How will the people involved feel if this continues?

- How will I feel?

- How will my child feel?

It's easiest to practice ACT looking at the recent past. For example, think of a pattern you followed yesterday and evaluate it. In what ways was that pattern helpful? In what ways was it destructive?

You can use a simple matrix to help you practice ACT. *Costs* are the undesired effects, downside, or risks. *Benefits* are the upsides or desired effects. For example, you are trying to decide between going on a family road trip or taking a staycation at home.

	Costs	Benefits
Road trip		
Staycation		

This ACT matrix encourages you to consider a decision's impact now and into the future, for you and your child. For example, you child asks you to buy her a new computer game:

	Short-term implications of buying the game	Long-term implications of buying the game
For kid(s)		
For parent(s)		

You can adapt how the matrix looks at consequences for you and others. For example, maybe you are thinking about changing jobs, and you want to consider how that would affect your family.

	Costs	Benefits
Me		
My family		

You can also make a matrix to experiment evaluating both practical and emotional components of a decision:

	Costs	Benefits
Emotional		
Practical		

In any of these matrices, remember the key idea of blending thinking and feeling (your own and others').

ACT in Real Time

In the example above, I encouraged you to think of a situation from the recent past (an incident yesterday) or a decision for the future (where to go on vacation). The bigger challenge is to apply consequential thinking in the moment.

You're in the midst of getting ready for dinner. Your child, who has loved peas for years, sees what you're cooking and declares with certainty: "Peas are gross." What's your pattern in this moment?

Now that you know about ACT, you pause for just six seconds. You evaluate. Then you decide how to respond. What will it be?

"Fine, brat, then you cook dinner" probably isn't your ideal response (though, who knows, that might work sometimes). Yet you might be feeling just that way.

It's one thing to apply consequential thinking and know that your pattern or reaction isn't optimal. It's quite another to make the change to something new. One reason is that the emotions that were pushing on the pattern are still there. Let's deal with that part of the equation.

Remember the key idea of blending thinking and feeling (your own and others')

Navigate Emotions

Emotions push and pull us all the time. It reminds me of sailing on San Francisco Bay with my stepdad, Hank (who I met when I was three years old), on a stormy and cold day when I was about ten. The U.S. Navy ship on which he served was in port, so we were sailing out to see her. The winds came whipping around Angel Island and bounced off the hills, waves frothed back and forth, and everything was drenched. We were skimming along, but the rigging was screaming under so much tension I thought the whole mast was going to break apart. The boat tipped over so far that "standing up" required putting my feet on what was normally the side of the boat.

I was terrified. Yet somehow all this force was (barely) contained, channeled into rocketing us forward. Hank was at the tiller, and he had to shout for me to hear him, just three feet away. But I could hear the joy in his voice at the raw energy of this moment, and as we worked that boat through the bluster, it became thrilling fun.

As I discussed in Part I, emotions are chemically encoded signals that serve as an internal feedback system. They focus us and galvanize us to deal with both opportunities and threats. They are packets of energy plus data coursing through our bodies and affecting every living cell.

Just as Hank was navigating our little sailboat, moving intentionally through the windy bay, we can move through the complexity of emotions. Just as the wind and waves propelled our boat, emotions can propel us. Just as we had to set the sails right to capture that energy, we need to set ourselves up to capture emotional energy. Just as we needed to keep adjusting the sails with changing conditions, we need to be agile in real life. And just as the power of the storm demanded our most careful sailing, big emotions require careful handling.

Big emotions come up a lot when we're in conflict with our kids. They come up when kids are in transition. And they come up from watching movies or reading books – we have many opportunities to practice.

THE FOREST

The story we tell ourselves changes our emotional experience of a situation. We literally change our brains when we make up a different story. "My kid is an idiot" produces one set of brain chemicals. "My kid is playful" produces another.

When Emma was four and a half, I read her read *Little House on the Prairie*, and then I started to read her *Little House in the Big Woods*. One weekend, instead of our usual outing to the beach, Emma lobbied for a trip to the woods.

As we drove into The Forest of Nicene Marks State Park in California, Emma kept telling Max not to be scared – in that way that makes the other person feel scared.

Emma was creating drama in the backseat, talking about the spooky trees and then reassuring her brother. "Don't worry, I got ya." Then Emma asked, "See these fish?" pointing to the decals on her window, "These are 'fighter fighter' [fire fighter] fish. They'll protect you."

Max did not seem scared at all, but he enjoyed Emma's attention.

When we left the car and started walking through the trees, Emma pointed to the butterfly on her shirt and said, "Max, this is a powerful butterfly. It will be poison to any mean animals, but not to nice ones, so you don't have to be scared."

Emma's assurances were probably more for her own sake than for her brother's, but the choice to focus on protecting him, the story she was choosing to tell about the experience, transformed her emotional reality.

I was struck by the power of her magical thinking. A four-year-old redefined her world as a way to change her feelings. And, of course, it worked. The "magic" of magical thinking is that beliefs shape our experience of the world. Rather than feel fear, Emma chose to experience power.

First, her imagination created the fear based on some past stories (probably seeing the scary wolves in "Beauty and the Beast"). Often we stop there, and we keep recreating the past because we believe that's the way the world is. But Emma demonstrated a powerful way to navigate emotions: use compassion and imagination to change the story.

Both kids said their favorite part of the trip was climbing up from the river. They each negotiated the steep path without my help (except my foot strategically placed next to Max's each time he started to slip, but don't tell him that).

They both experienced the victory of a challenge just beyond what felt possible. Again, there is power just in reaching – in stretching. Succeed or fail, you are more fully alive when you have to climb with hands and feet.

As you stretch and engage in the challenges of being a parent, give yourself permission to imagine that you have all the power you need. Find someone to protect and nurture, and let that galvanize you to create a new possibility. Change the story to change your perception of different situations, and your emotions will also change.

Uncover Layers

One fact about emotions: We almost always have several at the same time. I can be fighting with my son, and at the very same time love him beyond measure, feel guilty for my fighting, feel totally fed up with him not listening to me, and...and...and....It's a paradox: Several opposing elements existing simultaneously. They don't cancel each other out; they swirl around each other.

It's all too easy, however, to let one emotion dominate like the loud kid on the playground making us play dodge ball again.

One of the simplest ways to transform an emotion is to observe the multiple feelings and then to focus on the one that is most useful. You're angry with your child, and you love her or him. Both at the same time. (In fact, you probably wouldn't even be angry if the love weren't also there. When we care more, we feel more.)

> "
>
> One fact about emotions: We almost always have several at the same time.
>
> "

When I'm mad at one of the kids, it's easy for me to become even angrier by giving attention to all the problems, the barriers, the struggles. If I'm also feeling love at the same time, what would happen if I placed my attention on what I love about my child?

When you begin to notice that you have multiple, paradoxical feelings, it will help you navigate your emotions. Because anger and love exist simultaneously, you may find it's not all that difficult to shift from one to another. The next challenge is to shift *without* discounting or suppressing or denying the other. Let them both exist. Hold them both as precious messages.

The way we think about our own feelings, and feel about our own thoughts, has incredible power. Remember the brain is constantly reforming, constantly changing itself, constantly adapting to efficiently do the work you put in front of it.

THE NEUROSCIENCE OF NAVIGATING

I love this quote from Gandhi:

As human beings, our greatness lies not so much in being able to remake the world – that is the myth of the atomic age – as in being able to remake ourselves.

In the last decades, we've learned so much about how the brain works. We now know that Gandhi was right not only at a philosophical level but also at a neurological level.

Let's step back and take a more in-depth look at how our brains work. We talked about the amygdala, the "reaction center" that's triggered primarily by perceived threat to ourselves and now, as parents, our children. Just like the rest of our brain which changes itself as we learn, the amygdala is "programmed" by our experiences and the stories we tell ourselves about each experience.

Our brains store all of our learning in neural networks: constellations of brain cells interconnected so that they fire together. These webs of neural connections are constantly changing, weaving and reweaving a map of the world and the way to move through it. The points of inter-connection are made through branches, called *dendrites*, that nearly touch, creating a small gap called a synapse.

Six amazingly powerful points about your brain and emotions:

1. Billions of opportunities.

We have billions of brain cells, and each has numerous dendrites reach-ing out in a web to form trillions upon trillions of synapses. There is a vast – mind-bogglingly huge – number of synapses in every brain. The lowest estimate I've seen is 100,000,000,000,000 (that's 14 zeros). The highest estimate I've seen is 1 with 800 zeroes – I suspect that's more than there are grains of sand on the planet.

As parents, we are mapping our relationships with our child into these complex networks of thought and emotion.

2. Fire together, wire together.

Brain cells link up because they begin to fire together – one concept, or map, suddenly becomes associated with another. As that happens, more dendrites begin to interconnect increasing the efficiency and power of the linkage. When that association is interrupted, dendrites begin to disconnect.

Every time we think of a child as stubborn, we're creating more neu-ral interconnections to associate her with that idea. Yet our brains are adaptable, and we can change the way they're wired.

3. Dendrites move.

It takes about one ten-thousandth of a second for a dendrite to move and reconnect somewhere else. There is a constant reprogramming happening – and it's biological. Our brain changes itself. We change our own physiology.

We have wired reactions to our kids. But when we take just a moment to listen to our children or to observe something new, we change our brains and can rewire our reactions.

4. Synapses optimize.

In Part I, we talked about how each neurohormone has a unique key shape, one for every emotion. Those "keys" look for matching "locks" on the surface of every cell in your body. The surface of a dendrite will actually change to form more receptor sites to match the "keys" that are frequently crossing that particular synapse – the brain is increasing its efficiency.

If you "practice" losing your patience with a child, your brain gets better and better at impatience. If you practice compassion, your brain gets better and better at that.

5. Emotions regulate.

A major function of emotion is to create readiness in the brain. Readiness for combat, intimacy, learning, etc. You bathe your brain in emotions and set it up to focus and respond in a particular way.

If you are thinking about how impossible it is to be a parent, and you're bathing your brain in feelings of inadequacy, you're setting your whole body up to respond with fight, flee, or freeze. Different thoughts and emotions can set you up to connect, learn, grow, and celebrate.

6. Stories transform.

The brain is self-regulating, and the stories you tell yourself become real to your brain. You can actually make yourself forget by telling yourself something is unimportant. You can easily make yourself enraged by telling yourself someone is bad. You can create peace by telling a different story.

It makes a difference how you think about yourself as a parent, and how you think about your partner and your children. See the good and cherish it.

Taken together, these facts lead me to a simple, stunning conclusion: I am who I choose to be.

Yes, there is huge component of nature and of luck. I was born at a particular point in time to particular parents in a particular place. Because of my privilege, it was dramatically more likely for me to get a good education, to become concerned with making the world better, and to not experience true desperation. My height and eye color and skin color are fixed.

There are many, many things that happen in the world around me that affect me and are, at least in large part, beyond my control. What's in the water I drink and air I breathe. If my baby has colic. If my wife or kids get sick. If I lose money on investments because of some out-of-the-blue event. If I win the jackpot when I put $1 in the slot machine. There is an element of randomness. In fact, new research shows that even the way our brain cells grow is partly chaotic – our dendrites grow partly due to genetics, partly due to environment, and partly from randomness.

But there are so many *more* things where I *do* have choice. What I think about. The way I use my energy. What I eat and how much and where and why. How I respond when my child cries or laughs. What investments I select. How often I put the dollar in the slot machine.

I don't get to choose everything. I don't get to control everything. But I get to choose what I do next – and, it turns out, I get to choose how I feel about it.

Chapter 5:

Creating New Possibilities

In the last chapter, I talked about applying consequential thinking (ACT) and navigating emotions, two of four skills needed to Choose Yourself in the model. ACT is like brakes on a car. It gives you a chance to pause before you act, even in the heat of the moment. As you learn to navigate emotions, you come to recognize that you can feel multiple emotions simultaneously and to realize that you have the power to change not only how you think but also how you feel. Navigating emotions is like steering the car.

In this chapter, I look at two more skills for choosing yourself: intrinsic motivation and optimism. Both focus on moving forward. Intrinsic motivation is like the car's engine, and optimism is the gas you put in the tank.

Choosing Yourself is hard work. Maintaining the status quo and following comfortable-but-problematic patterns are far easier. Intrinsic motivation helps you find the energy required for self-management.

Engage Intrinsic Motivation

Motivation can come from external or internal influences. When we try to motivate ourselves and our children, we have a choice between the two.

Focusing on external factors, we can create some measure of compliance. For example, we can constantly remind our kids to say "please," in hopes that some day they'll do it without reminders and mean it. This is a *behaviorist* approach popularized by psychologist B.F. Skinner. Behaviorists think that people are primarily motivated by external forces, and we can get people to do whatever we want if we apply the right levers. Does the name Pavlov ring a bell?

External, or *extrinsic*, motivators are forces from the outside. Giving your child a treat, sticker, or gold star is extrinsic because the source of the reward comes from outside the child. The same is true of externally enforced consequences or threats of consequence, such as punishments.

Internal or *intrinsic* motivation comes from within. It's based on values, identity, vision, and relationships. Intrinsic motivation is driven by emotion, by wanting to feel good about our choices. It's a lot more complex and slow to build. Because intrinsic motivation, by nature, is a force from inside a person, someone else can't control it. We don't get to control our child's internal motivation, but we do have tremendous influence as our children develop their intrinsic motivation.

If we simply want our kids to comply and do what they're told, extrinsic threats and rewards can work, at least in the short term. Research suggests that for rote actions like "pick up your toys," or "say please," behaviorism can be fairly effective. If your goal is *only* to have your children keep their room clean or to have them use polite words, you can probably get them to comply through a scheme of rewards and punishments (at least temporarily).

The direct, simple application of external influence can be quite appealing. That's probably why behaviorism remains very common. Many parenting books, most schools, and almost all corporate sales departments rely on it. There is a very big problem though: It works only for behavior.

In other words, when approaching motivation, consider your goals. Are you looking for the behavior of *say please* (irrespective of meaning it), or are you looking for an internal attitude of respect? Are you satisfied with the behavior of sharing (even if hostile), or is the feeling of care your real goal? When you want your child to pick up toys, are you looking for a clean floor, or are your actually concerned about the value of responsibility?

Here's the kicker: When you "motivate" children via rewards and punishments, they may comply with the behaviors, but research shows *you will reduce their commitment to the internal attitudes, feelings, and values*. For more on this, check out work by Alfie Kohn, such as his book *Unconditional Parenting*, and Carol Dweck, who wrote *Mindset* (and in the business sector, Dan Pink's *DRIVE* provides an in-depth look at the science of motivation).

In other words, if all you care about is behavior, carrots and sticks are your friends. For example, when potty training, you might have a pretty simple goal: pee in the toilet. You might not care if he respects the toilet or is self-motivated – the behavior is the goal. On the other hand, when you're looking at more complex issues, like caring and respect, you may need a radically different approach.

Thinking to the future, if you want your children to learn about the internal assets that will make them women and men of character – courage, compassion, integrity, passion, humility, discipline, creativity, gratitude – then the carrots and sticks are not for you. Again: as we increase the focus on external forces (rewards and punishments), internal factors dim.

The same dynamic occurs for motivating yourself. When you are trying to "make yourself do something" it's completely different from when you *want* to do something. Emotion is the secret to motivating yourself.

Let's say you want to be healthier, but you like eating French fries. It's lunchtime, and you see fries on the menu. Do you order them? It depends which has more emotional power: your desire for fries now, or your image of a healthier you sometime in the future (or perhaps more powerful: your goal to be healthy so that you stay around for your kids). Remember, emotion drives attention and motivates action – if we have two options, and one has more emotional power, it wins.

When you want to motivate, build emotional energy connected with a vision or goal, so that moving ahead is emotionally enticing.

The ability to engage intrinsic motivation is invaluable in thinking about your motivation – and your kids'. It turns out that the two are tightly intertwined.

When you are trying to "make yourself do something" it's completely different from when you *want* to do something. Emotion is the secret to motivating yourself.

"BECAUSE I SAID SO"

A frequent refrain I hear from parents (and in my own head), is: *Why don't my kids do what they are supposed to do?*

I'm willing to be a very patient parent about substantive issues, but I lose it when arguments ensue over about trivial issues, such as what shoes four-year-old Emma will wear today. In this situation, I suspect, I see an issue as unimportant, and my child sees the same issue as vital. I am impatient because of my assessment, and she is baffled by my impatience.

Lesson one: Just because it is obvious to you does not make it obvious to your kids – and just because it is important to you does not make it important to them.

What leads people to "do what they're supposed to do"? If you go to work and are told to follow some arcane procedure, are you motivated? Is it enough to know the rule? Some people seem to be satisfied with that, and they'll go along. Others, most of us, I suspect, want a bit more to go on. We want tasks to make sense. We want to know that the work we're doing has meaning, and the people we serve are not wasting our lives. So we ask, "Why?" And we work harder when there is an answer that resonates with us.

When I was a child, I often would challenge my dad's authority by asking, *why do I have to?* His most frequent answer, "Because I said so!" His words and tone caused me to stop asking because I was afraid. I swore I'd never talk to my children that way.

As a two-year-old, my Max liked to say, "Why?" to just about everything! Usually it was his way of interacting, rather than challenging, almost a habitual way of engaging in dialogue. Still, much to my chagrin, I found myself saying, "Because I said so!"

"Max, pick up those toys."

"Why Daddy?"

"Because they are messy."

"Why?"

"Well, because you threw them on the floor."

"Why?"

"Let's just clean up now. I'll help you."

Often the dialogue continued in the same vein until Max finally said, "Oh, I see." Or I just gave up!

I realized that Max's quest for "Why?" was *insatiable*. As it is supposed to be! Understanding the landscape is one of the most important jobs for a preschooler. Like most of us, he was seeking to understand his purpose and his relationship with the world – he was seeking meaning.

Lesson Two: People want to understand the point.

For Max, just having dialogue and partnership – having me participate in cleaning up alongside him – created enough meaning (usually) for him to clean up his toys. That's one reason modeling behavior is so important, especially for parents: If you are important, what you do is important. And as the parent, you will always be of the utmost importance to your children, even if they act otherwise (this is sometimes hard to remember with two teens). You create meaning simply by participating or even just being there. For your child, meaning also comes from simply belonging to the family, interacting socially with parents or siblings, and doing things together.

Lesson Three: Relationships motivate.

Another challenge in "getting people to do what they're supposed to do" is even harder to handle. Who decides what kids are "supposed to do"? Do you want to motivate your kids to figure out what to do, or do you want them to be obedient and do what you want? It turns out the two are, to some degree, in conflict.

Motivation is about hooking into that inner sense of purpose. It's about connecting with an individual's goals, interest, and values. This "fire within" is what I want my children to develop now and for the future.

Obedience is about compliance. It's about ensuring that kids know who has the power to reward and punish, and finding what they'll respond to. Obedience grows from greed for external rewards, fear of punishments, or threat of disapproval.

With my kids, I often have moments where I wish they'd just obey me. In those moments, I think, *I should be stricter, less flexible, or even scarier.* Then I think about the other lesson that I'd teach through this approach. I struggle to hold onto long-term goals in those moments. I want my kids to grow up to lead through passion and vision, not through fear and intimidation, so I need to model that. I want my kids to grow up to challenge inequity, to search for higher truth, to quest for life's deeper meaning, which means they must see me do the same.

One time when Emma was "being disobedient," maybe around three years old, I thought: *If I could give her a pill right now that would make her obey, but she'd be obedient all her life, would I do it?* The answer was clearly no. Imagining the long term helped me see the present more clearly. I want her to continue to be someone who challenges authority. I need to remember that her asserting power is something valuable, not something bad. That said, teachers and other authorities might not embrace this attribute as quickly as do her mom and dad. It's a balancing act: teaching our kids to follow rules and be considerate of others, and when and how to challenge rules respectfully.

Lesson four: We actually want our kids to have power.

To recap the four points for parenting motivation:

1. *Just because it's obvious to you does not make it obvious to your kids – and just because it is important to you does not make it important to them.* How can you help your kids value what you value? How can you help yourself value what your kids value?

2. *People want to understand the point.* Can you recognize when dissent is actually misunderstanding, and use that as an opportunity for teaching?

3. *Relationships motivate.* How can you put time and energy into participating with your kids in things that you want them to be motivated about?

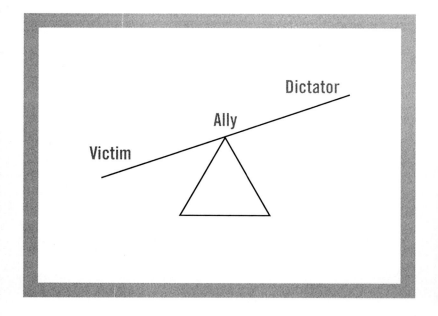

4. *We want our kids to have power*. What if you see their use of power as a signal of positive strength? How can you provide opportunities for your child to responsibly exercise power?

Power is a central ingredient in the parent–child relationship. The fourth lesson – *we want our kids to have power* – is complex and important. Do you push for obedience? Is that what you really want? Can you see how your own reactions take power from your kids?

Here's a simple way to think about power as a parent.

Choosing a Role: Victim, Ally, or Dictator

Another way of exploring intrinsic motivation is to evaluate the words you use – what you tell yourself and what you tell your children – and how those reflect your use of power.

Often people use victim statements: *I can't. They made me. I had no choice*. These words give up power. They position others as responsible for our choices.

At the other extreme are dictator words: You *have to, must,* or *should*. These words signal taking power away from someone else.

Suppose I tell my kids: "You have no choice. You have to eat your broccoli."

While there's nothing innately wrong with my broccoli conviction, let's look at the power dynamic. I'm claiming that I have all the power in this situation. Maybe I do. Maybe I'm willing to go to the mat for broccoli, let them eat nothing until they finally cave in. But the other lesson here is quite risky.

After all, what's my real goal? Am I looking for short-term obedience, or something long-term and deeper? Do I want them to eat broccoli, or is that just shorthand for wanting them to have good health habits and the flexibility and openness to try new things? If it's the latter, then a broccoli battle is not going to get me to my real goals.

15 Ways to Recharge

A lot of activities that young children like are really boring for adults, but some are fun for both of you. Do more of the latter.

Teach your child to enjoy the music you enjoy.

Time spent in prayer or meditation makes you more efficient later.

Listen to great audiobooks in the car.

Put your hands in soil, even if it's just a little window box garden.

Go on dates.

If you have more than one child, schedule fun time with one at a time. It's a treat for them and for you.

Get a massage or pamper yourself once in awhile.

If you can get yourself to an ocean, listen to the waves and feel the sand.

Do not tell yourself that yoga, walking, or exercise is "taking time away." If it gives you energy or reduces stress, it serves an important purpose. Plus you're modeling a healthy lifestyle

Talk about the future and your dreams. Ask your children about their dreams.

Cook and eat amazing food.

Serve others.

Sit under a tree and watch the leaves.

Give yourself a gift of a few minutes of doing nothing.

If I take power and say, *you have to*, then I'm also giving my child a message: *you are powerless*. That's going to backfire when I want him to become self-motivated.

Important note: The victim stance and dictator stance are interconnected. When one person shifts to dictator, she is demanding someone else shift to victim. When someone chooses victimhood, he is leaving a void that someone has to fill as a dictator.

Think of it like an old-fashioned seesaw. When one side goes up, the other goes down. But the middle stays pretty much still. The middle ground is where being an *ally* resides.

When you use the power of being an ally, you don't take others' power or give up your own. It's a place of enduring strength. To take that position with your child, carefully consider your use of power – don't give away your own power and let the child be a dictator. Don't take away your child's power.

What does it sound like? Allies use phrases such as: *One option is... Have you considered...? My preference is... How can we...?* Ally language is closer to neutral. It's about observations vs. judgments; questions vs. declarations.

FUELING YOUR INTERNAL MOTIVATION

Parents are quite motivated by biology. We're hardwired to care about our kids. But it's hard. It's exhausting, and often the rewards are far away (I've heard that being a grandparent is one of those rewards, let's circle back to this in a couple decades, ok?)

This is one reason self-care is so important for parents. It's a bit cliché to talk about "me time," and maybe used as an excuse for self-indulgence... but in a healthy balance, it's important. *What are you doing to recharge your batteries?* On the left page there are 15 strategies that have worked for me, maybe some will entice you.

Hopefully at least one of these will help you recharge!

RECAP: CHOOSE YOURSELF SKILLS

In Part II, we've been looking at the skills needed to Choose Yourself. To responding intentionally instead of reacting on autopilot.

In chapter 4, "From Reaction to Response," we talked about how to:

- *Apply consequential thinking (ACT)*: Pause and look ahead to see if you're creating the results you want.

- *Navigate emotions*: Use emotions to move forward in a positive way.

We applied consequential thinking to evaluate and maybe decide to change a pattern. As we learned to navigate emotions, we tuned in, listened, and identified other feelings to help us step forward.

In chapter 5, "Creating New Possibilities," we talked about how to:

- *Engage intrinsic motivation*: Tap into drivers such as safety, belonging, achievement, and purpose to create powerful commitment.

While exploring the concept of *intrinsic motivation*, we looked at the concepts of motivation vs. obedience, and how to be your child's ally, not a dictator or a victim.

To Choose Yourself, there's one more essential skill. Supposed you've come through all the steps so far and want to try something new instead of an old pattern, but you don't see any other options? If we don't believe we have options, we'll stick with an old pattern. We need a way to generate new solutions. We need to:

Exercise optimism: Create new options to solve challenges.

Exercise Optimism

Optimism is often misunderstood to mean, "pretend everything is fine, no mater what the reality is." Others respond to this false cheer saying, "Be realistic." Genuine optimism *is* realistic. It means facing reality *and* knowing you can make it better. You can't do everything, but you can do something.

This skill is essential for Choosing Yourself because without optimism, you won't find alternatives to your patterns. With pessimism, you see no options. With optimism, you create options.

Optimism includes both emotional and cognitive components. You choose to feel optimistic, and this helps you think optimistically. The result is powerful. Research shows those who use a more optimistic style live longer, are healthier, and have more career success, better relationships, and more life satisfaction.

THE SUN IS NEW EACH DAY

"The sun is new each day."

–Heraclitus (ca 500 BCE)

At around six months old, Emma woke up each morning laughing and smiling, even when she had a grumpy night or driven us to the brink by refusing to go to sleep. At that time, I asked a group of 12-year-olds if there is a lesson in Emma's morning cheerfulness. Their answers ran a gamut.

"Be optimistic because that's more satisfying."

"Live in the present because this moment is all you have."

"When you are a baby, you don't remember the bad things."

"If you get enough sleep, you are happy."

"You really love her."

"If you start with smiling, then the people you care about will be happy."

As Patty and I talked to the 12-year-olds, and later to each other, I found more and more lessons in Emma's morning joy.

Patty reminded me that as a teacher it is hard to let students start fresh each day because expectations, frustrations, positives, and negatives build up. But with Emma, she said, "We give each other the gift of total forgiveness. Even if the night before I was so mad that I wanted to scream, the morning is a new start."

In most areas of our lives, people around us know us a certain way. In school, teachers look at a child's file and "know" who is a good student, who is a "discipline problem," etc. In life, people around us, even our families, "know" that we fit into a particular template. They've seen our patterns, expect us to behave a particular way, and treat us as if that's how we'll act.

One of my favorite quotes from Anabel Jensen, Six Seconds' president, is, "Treat people the way you want them to be." For me, maybe that's the lesson that Emma was teaching me each bubbly morning. "Hey, Daddy, I know you are happy to be awake and playing with me," she seemed to say. And most mornings, I was.

Another lesson for me is that while I practice living in the moment, the pain passes. In the 16+ years since those mornings, there have been wonderful days and brutal ones. The fighting about bedtime, the arguments about getting dressed in the morning, or eating peas vs. throwing them, those all faded. What remains clear and bright in my memory is how we'd wake up to Emma kicking us and laughing, to her smiling just from seeing us in a new day.

CUSTOMER (AND DADDY) DELIGHT

When I've given presentation to people who work in customer service, we often talk about customer "delight" and exceeding expectations. Businesses have a terrible time creating real loyalty, truly capturing the heart and mind of customers (and employees), but it may be the most valuable aspect of a successful organization.

For me, *delight* is one of those wonderful words redolent with richness and emotional pull – in part because of my son.

Max, or "Maxie Boy" as he called himself as a preschooler, found delight around every corner. I vividly remember his delight when he was learning to walk. I can still see his face as he jumped off the arm of couch over and over, sprawling onto the cushions and smiling.

Maybe my delight in Maxie's delight is one of those hardwired responses that help parents nurture their children. I can think of no greater pleasure than seeing my children truly delighted.

I was talking to a client at Disney World about how the company creates a sense of wonder. She said all she needs to do to make a parent's day is come up to a child and play along with the fantasy – for example, with one of the hundreds of little girls in a Cinderella dress, saying, "Oh, is that you Cinderella? What a beautiful dress you have on today!" She said the kids light up, and in turn the parents do too.

That's what would happen when Max would run around the beach and then come bounding toward me splashing along the edge of the water. Still today, when he turns that 1,000-watt smile toward me, my heart overflows with wonder and appreciation. I frequently tell my children, "Thank you for letting me be your Daddy." In Maxie's glow, I am more fully alive.

There is something powerfully contagious about simple joy. And as parents, we have a million opportunities to appreciate it by simply enjoying a moment with our child.

Research suggests an important link between gratitude and optimism. When we can see abundance (even in hard times), it strengthens the muscle of optimism. We're more able to see multiple perspectives and identify choices. When we feel lucky to be ourselves, honored to be the ones called Mommy or Daddy, we're able to see, and even create, more possibilities to be worthy of the title.

Gratitude is an emotional doorway to increased optimism. To increase gratitude, practice. Tonight at bedtime, tell your children ten things you appreciate about them. I used to do this when the kids were little, and I could see my affirmations settle over them like a blanket. At the same time, I'd walk away from that moment more recharged, more capable, and more open to tomorrow's potential.

USING OPTIMISM

In this section, I use the phrases *using optimism*, or *practicing optimism*. It's common to consider someone as an optimist or pessimist, but this implies a fixed state. As Martin Seligman (one of the preeminent researchers in the area of optimism) explained in his book *Learned Optimism*, optimism is a style, and we can learn to use it more. Optimism is a learned way of explaining successes and failures.

This is an optimistic view of optimism! We can develop more skill and ease in using an optimistic approach. And, even if we're frequently optimistic, sometimes we all find the voice of pessimism creeping in. As parents, one of the greatest gifts we can give our children is the skill of optimism. It's learned – which means we can influence our kids to strengthen this muscle.

Sphere of Control

One simple idea for exercising optimism relates to an idea in the first part of this chapter: Recognize the limits of your own power. This may sound pessimistic, but it's not. When people use optimism, they take ownership of their responsibility, but they don't try to fix everything. Stephen Covey discusses this in his landmark book *Seven Habits of*

Highly Effective People. We need to know the difference between our sphere of influence and our sphere of control.

Within our sphere of control are those things we can directly affect. In my experience, these are limited to my own thoughts, feelings, and actions, such as what I say to my kids and how I say it, how much time I spend with my kids, and what behaviors I model when we're together.

Our sphere of influence is a much larger area. We can all influence others. How I talk to my kids changes how they feel and behave. If I encourage them to do their homework in advance and they do, it makes the day before the assignment is due much more pleasant for the whole family. I can't make them do their homework, but I can make sure they have time and space to do it.

When you are finding yourself being pessimistic, it's likely that you are trying to control outcomes that are not in your sphere of control. If I felt pessimistic about my daughter ever learning to be patient with her brother, perhaps I'm forgetting that I can't control this. (More cause for optimism: At 16 and 14, they are generally loving toward one another.)

By making this simple distinction between what I can control and what I can influence, I have power. Not control. I can make choices that may work. If they don't work, I can make more choices.

Disputing

One more tip for exercising optimism from Martin Seligman. I interviewed him many years ago, and I asked him how someone could shift from pessimism. He said, "You need to hear your own pessimism and argue with yourself." In Seligman's model, a *pessimistic voice* will talk about three aspects of a problem:

Time: It will last forever. It's permanent.

Isolation: It will affect everything. It's pervasive.

Effort: There is nothing you can do. You're powerless.

When you are practicing pessimism, you tell yourself some or all of these three Ps (permanent, pervasive, powerless).

Now imagine you are in a conversation. You tell some person about a challenge you're having with your child. That person replies: "Your child is never going to get better, she is going to ruin her whole life, and there is nothing you can do about it." Do you just nod your head and accept that? Probably not. Probably you say, "Wait a minute, bud. First, nothing is forever. Second, there are a lot of things she's good at, and third, there is plenty I can do to help her."

In other words, you are likely to challenge, or *dispute*, this person's argument. What Seligman pointed out is that when we tell ourselves these very same things, we take them as truths and we don't argue with ourselves.

The trick is to notice the voice of pessimism in your own head and challenge yourself. Ask yourself: *Is there another way to think about this?*

In the model, we use the phrase *exercise optimism* because it's work. It takes effort to actively seek out sources of gratitude. There's sweat involved in challenging your own assumptions and seeking out new perspectives. But the effort is well worthwhile. It will help you create more possibilities for yourself and in your parenting, and it will allow you to teach your children this critical element of resilience.

Chapter 6: Helping Your Children Choose Themselves

From the previous two chapters, I hope you're coming to believe that in order for your children to learn to Choose *Themselves* – to be more accountable for their own lives – your primary job is to Choose *Yourself*. You'll see how this works in a few minutes when you read about emotional Aikido and the "first rule of emotional intelligence." The point now is that when we Choose Ourselves, we create an opportunity for our kids to do the same.

If I want my child to be self-motivated, I need to reduce my use of extrinsic motivators. If you want your child to stop getting into silly power struggles, get out of those silly power struggles yourself. If we want children to be resilient and show grit, we need to do the hard work to exercise our own optimism more frequently.

At the same time as we're doing the work ourselves, there are a host of powerful strategies we can use to help our kids develop these emotional intelligence skills. The theme of this chapter is autonomy: *An essential ingredient for a child to learn to Choose Herself is the autonomy to do so.*

Here are some milestones to work toward at various ages:

Self-Management Goals

Ages 0–4: Recognize that you are making choices, and your choices have an effect. Learn that feelings can help you, but they are not in charge of you.

Ages 5–7: Learn to think about the costs and benefits of your choices, and practice talking about how you make choices and delay gratification. Learn that when you have many feelings, you can choose which to focus on. Understand that you have choice about how you express emotions. Learn the meaning of *optimism*.

Ages 8–11: Practice pausing to assess consequences *before* acting. Learn to step back from your own emotions and think about your feelings. Begin to recognize personal values and passions that motivate. Increase capacity to cooperatively interact with peers and at the same time compete physically and intellectually in positive ways.

Ages 12-15: Develop a sense of responsibility for your own choices. Identify yourself as someone who has both freedom and responsibility for making decisions. Practice listening to your own feelings as messages and shifting between multiple feelings.

Ages 16+: Take ownership of your own choices as someone with self-efficacy and self-determination. Develop passion and commitment to fuel inner motivation. Actively practice to create an optimistic perspective.

IN A GENTLE WAY YOU CAN SHAKE THE WORLD

Consider these two lists about change:

Make change		Create a new context
Push it through		Shift
Pull them along		Realign
Reorganize	vs.	Model new behaviors
Blow things up		Observe the potential
Shake them up		Share new meaning
Work on it		Nourish

Before our kids were born, people kept saying things to me like, "Oh, nothing will be the same." "You don't know what you are in for." "This is the end of 'just the two of you.'" They were all right, and all wrong.

They were right because parenthood radically changed my thinking, feeling, and acting. They were all wrong because the implication was that I would be forced to change, I was losing something, and I would resent it.

Emma and Max changed my life simply by being so present and important. They changed my life without doing anything, without pushing anything. They did not exert power over me; rather they created a new context.

Perhaps that is part of what Gandhi meant when he said:

"In a gentle way you can shake the world."

One of the most profound lessons fatherhood has taught me is that when I push and demand, I get resistance. Instead, in the small moments of parenthood, I can choose to have the best version of me step forward, for instance, in the role of my children's ally. In so doing, I invite them to do the same.

This reminds me of when, as a teen, I studied Aikido, a Japanese martial art. In Aikido, instead of directly opposing a force, you move to stand next to your opponent. Why? Because when you are in direct opposition, the force you exert is directly opposed – the impact is severe, and it requires tremendous power.

This Aikido principle applies to emotions and relationships. When we directly oppose, we actually strengthen opposition. I've come to see this as "the first rule of emotional intelligence":

When people feel pushed, they resist.

Here's a simple test: *If your child is resisting, are you pushing?* It's tough to stop pushing! Recently, I was talking to a colleague about a recurring homework argument with Max. I said, "I told him really nicely." My colleague said: "What would happen if you were *asking*, instead of telling?" Aha! I was pushing.

The big challenge of parenting with emotional intelligence is to make that Aikido move to stand side-by-side. Choose Yourself so your child can do the same. Let's explore how to practice emotional Aikido.

Tools for Choosing

Try these strategies to create a context for children to learn to Choose Themselves:

Force field. As you're thinking about changes you want to see in your children, ask yourself: What kind of force am I exerting? Is it a force of compassion, joy, frustration, fear? There are many kinds of power we can assert.

Change the game. Just as our children have indirectly created change in our lives, gently shaking our world, how can you change the situation or the context, so your child responds in new ways?

The first rule of emotional intelligence. *When people feel pushed, they resist.* If you notice your child is resisting, check to see if you are pushing.

TIME-OUT

One morning when she was about four, Emma told me about a book that she had just read. "It's about parents who screamed at their kids because the kids were bad."

I was quite worried.

"Emma, do your Momma and Daddy scream at you and Maxie a lot?"

"No." (Big feeling of relief!)

"Are you and Maxie bad?"

"No, we're good. Sometimes we do bad stuff," she said. We'd been working on talking about how people sometimes make choices that don't work out very well.

"Like what?"

"Sometimes I push Maxie, and sometimes Maxie throws toys, and sometimes..."

Later, I asked Emma what parents should do when their kids make bad choices. She said the parents could just walk away.

"Don't the parents have to teach the kids not to make those choices?"

"Well, the kids could go on time-out."

"And what if that doesn't work?"

"The grownup could go on time-out too."

I am not sure if Emma was consciously recognizing that conflicts escalate because both parent and kids get heated up, but she's right. Conflict is mutual. Sometimes the most important intervention is for us to take a step away so we can navigate emotions. It's one of your most powerful emotional Aikido moves: *Step away.*

Tools for Reducing Conflict

As you're working to teach the skills of Choose Yourself, try these tips:

Label behavior. When you identify a problem, be sure to clearly articulate that it's the behavior or the choice that's a problem, not the child. *I like you. I don't like what you just did.*

Ask for advice. It's powerful to ask your children what they see as an appropriate response. This is not effective in the heat of conflict. Sometimes it's easier to talk about a third party: *If your friend Jane kept throwing her toys, what should her parents do?*

My time-out. Give yourself a gift of a moment to step away and re-think.

THAT'S *MY* (WHATEVER)

One of the most powerful techniques for navigating emotions is to validate a feeling. This means recognizing, accepting, and valuing it. Make your feeling an ally. This is easy with feelings like joy and trust. Not so much with feelings like jealousy and disappointment.

You can start practicing this with your kids. This is part of empathy, coming in Part III. You're connecting with your child in a different way to make space for her or him to navigate emotions. You become an emotional ally.

Anyone who has watched preschoolers has heard variations of: "That's *my* (whatever)." Jealousy is one of the core toddler experiences. Children's jealousy is a major challenge for most adults – perhaps in part because jealousy is also difficult for us as adults. One day when he was a bit younger than two years old, Max's best friend, Addison (aka "Addy Boy"), was over, and we conducted some unplanned experiments about this challenging feeling.

At that time, one of the central pillars of Max and Addy's friendship was their mutual delight in all things tractor. They both had toy tractors, tractor pajamas, tractor shoes, tractor Hot Wheels. It was a veritable construction yard here and across the street at Addy's house. They remained close friends for more than a decade. While Wii, Nerf, and skateboards and then sports and computers have replaced tractors, construction equipment was the foundation.

As sometimes happens when you're just over two feet tall, Addy was having a meltdown evening. In fact, for part of that evening, I had all three kids screaming and crying – a little stress test to make sure I really want to be a parent, I guess. My stress level was high anyway because Patty's estimated hour-long absence was stretching into the third hour.

Anyway, the evening became infinitely more pleasurable when, with no prodding on my part, Emma decided that comforting Addy would be her job. She kept getting up from the table saying, "I know, Daddy,"

Tools for Navigating Emotions

Here are three techniques to help practice *Emotional Aikido:*

Validate. If a child is expressing a feeling, recognize and name it. Don't try to change it (yet). Simply honor that she has this feeling.

Turn 180. Sometimes we need a jolt of creativity. Try doing the opposite of what you normally do, like agreeing when your child says, "That's *my* truck."

Turns vs. sharing. When you're under two feet tall, sharing is problematic. Taking turns is easier.

and bringing a toy or book to distract him.

Max was watching the scene from his high chair with two fists full of "bunny noodles," a slightly healthy version of macaroni and cheese. Every time Emma brought Addy a tractor or tractor book, Max began to shout.

"My book! That's MYYYYY BOOK!"

While I had an impulse to scream, I decided to be amused and curious instead. Rather than telling Max, *In our family we share* (a frequent family mantra), I decided to experiment with the opposite. Aikido!

"You're right, Maxie," I said seriously, "That *is* your book." (Insert pause for more shouting.) "Yes, it is yours. That's right."

The shouting diminished!

Then I said, "Addy's just having a turn" (volume increases from the high chair) – "And you can have it back in one minute. You will get your book back."

We repeated variations of this scenario for a good half hour, so I got to experiment with a few alternatives, and reinforcing Max's ownership (and letting Addy have all the toys and books) worked quite well.

My friend Ayman Sawaf says jealousy is a message about ownership. He says we feel jealous when we're not clear about our relationship with a thing or person, and it's a call to clarify who owns it. That's probably why Max felt such a stab of pain when Emma gave his treasured books to Addy. Max was not clear that they really were his. Especially when Emma, who acts like she owns everything, is the one giving the books away.

Adults tend to hear, "That's *my* (whatever)," as selfish and rude. Perhaps it would be more useful to hear is as a question: "Is that my (whatever)?" The one question will probably lead to others: Do I really want it? Am responsible for it? Why do I want it?"

HOW MANY BLOCKS?

One skill for navigating emotions is calibrating the correct response. Big problems might deserve a big response. Small ones, not so much. When Emma was around four years old, we had this discussion many times using building blocks.

"Emma, why are you shouting at your brother?"

"He keeps bothering me."

"Ah," I grab a few wooden blocks, "so how many blocks big is this problem?"

Emma starts stacking... "At *least* four."

"Hm. Did he break anything?"

"No."

"Did he hurt you?"

"No." Emma is starting to be less frustrated.

"So maybe the problem is just two blocks big?"

"I guess..."

Then we would go on to talk about how big her reaction was. Sometimes there was a five-block-tall reaction to a two-block problem.

Other times Emma helped me see that the problem was bigger than it looked from the outside. Often I made an assumption that she was overreacting, but when she could explain the scope of her hurt or frustration, I could see her perspective. Stacking blocks gave us a way to discuss the severity of the issue and a proportional response.

BUILDING CAPACITY

The toddler years were challenging, to say the least. At the same time, I have never experienced something as exciting as watching Emma and Max learn to do and be. They quickly became competent and opinionated in so many areas.

I remember cooking pancakes with Emma when she was two-and-a-half years old. She was getting good at cracking eggs (it involved cracking then squeezing hard – not *too* much shell ended up in the bowl), and we were working on stirring.

Making pancakes took nearly an hour. I could have done it myself in a few minutes. But this was time very well spent. Why? Because Emma and I were making something much more complex. We were making pancakes and *building capacity*. Ultimately, Emma was able to make pancakes herself; in fact, much better pancakes than I made.

Building capacity is about doing work in a way that allows more work to be accomplished in the future. In our lives, this happens in many ways. As parents, we take the time to show, rather than do it ourselves. As managers, we create systems and hire employees. As teachers, we build on previous skills to create new ones. We can also build our own capacity at home and at work. It's the essence of learning, and key for teaching our children autonomy.

To paraphrase author Madeline Levine: *The worst thing that parents can do for their children is something the kids can do for themselves. The second worst thing is doing something your kids can almost do for themselves.* When we're building capacity, we're preparing kids to do more for themselves.

Whose Childhood Is It?

We're in an era of two extremes: overparenting and underparenting. Overparenting is where we teach our children to be helpless by making life too easy. In his work on optimism, researcher Martin Seligman talks about *learned helplessness* as the opposite of optimism. Remember the victim–dictator dynamic: When we take more power, someone else (the child) becomes the victim.

One cause of overparenting is anxiety about the child's performance. If you are extremely concerned with the result (e.g., a letter grade in school), you might find yourself helping-to-an-extreme. As we know from Carol Dweck's research, this focus on the product (vs. process) creates significant issues for children's self-efficacy. If you want your child to be strong and know she's strong, she needs you to focus on the long game and recognize that she's building capacity, even (especially) when she fails.

Over or Under

If you've got a pattern of overparenting, ask yourself:

> Am I taking away my child's learning? (Even "way back" when I was a classroom teacher, sometimes parents forgot that it's their child's job to do the assignment. The parents had already completed middle school, now it was their kids' turn!)

> Am I building capacity? (If I do this, will my child be better equipped to do it herself/himself next week?)

> Am I showing my child I have complete faith in her ability to grow? (Sometimes we soften the challenge or save them from failure to the point where our children's other lesson is: *My parent doesn't think I can do this.*)

Underparenting is at least as destructive. It comes from being afraid of intimacy, overstressed, or just absent (either physically or by spending so much time on the computer or cell phone that you're not really in the room). You know you're underparenting when you rarely spend time with your children, or you think of yourself as a babysitter. Sometimes parents slip into underparenting because they want to be their child's friend. It's important and wonderful to have a friendly relationship, but you're the parent, not the pal.

Adding Complexity

When you create capacity, you also create new problems, including added complexity. Emma, Patty, and I built the capacity for Emma to put on shoes by herself, but she wouldn't leave her shoes on the outside porch, so the sandbox gradually migrated inside.

Business provides a simple example. You have three salespeople, and they are so busy, so you decide to hire a fourth. Of course, there's an initial investment because you start paying her day one, and she doesn't make many sales in the first quarter, maybe even the second. But eventually (we hope) she is bringing in more value than she's costing. You make that investment to build capacity. Unfortunately, the new person doesn't only add sales, but also adds complexity. She has her own opinions. She wants Pepsi in the fridge when the rest of the team likes Coke, but somehow you sort that out.

When you build capacity, you are dedicating some resources to that process. You're investing now to make things easier later. You also want to be sure you can use the capacity you build. Do you really need another salesperson? Is the investment and complexity worth it?

This cost–benefit analysis is like applying consequential thinking. In our day-to-day interactions with others, we need to evaluate the impact of our decisions. As parents, we need to apply consequential thinking about building capacity in our kids.

We decided the kids would help with chores, and through some trial and error, Max, starting at three years old, was assigned to help fold laundry. The first time it was a disaster. The second a cataclysm. The third a failure. The fourth a mess. But Patty persevered. Not because she really needed help with laundry. Not even because we think everyone should be able to wash and fold his own shirt (which is certainly a plus), but because we wanted to build Max's capacity. To give him a way to positively contribute to the family community.

Sometimes I feel frustrated with how long it takes for one of the kids to do a task because they're new at it. When I remind myself, "It's ok, we're building capacity," it helps me reframe the situation and remember that life is a process of learning, not a race to completion.

To help with the capacity-building process, let's look at the pancake example again. Here is a template for applying consequential thinking:

	Practical and emotional costs	Practical and emotional benefits
Short Term	Very messy, wasteful. Time investment. Stress.	Very fun for Emma, somewhat fun for me. Opportunity to chat and just be together.
Long Term	We don't want too many pancakes. Parents don't get to be the ones in charge.	Building positive connection and memories. Potential for breakfast in bed. Independence. Leverage pancake skills to other meals – dinner to follow?

Looking at this matrix, what's evident to me is that the decision to teach Emma to make pancakes was not motivated by the short term. Looking only at the short-term pros and cons, I would put her in front of *Blues Clues* and make pancakes myself. But applying consequential thinking requires balancing the short and long term – and looking at the long term, the story becomes clear: Build capacity.

There's another consideration. In corporate training, I often ask: *What's a time when your motivation at work increased a lot?* There are a range of fabulous answers, but one comes up a lot: *My manager encouraged me to stretch and do something that was a little beyond my skills or experience.* From this, I infer that the same formula works to help children to be intrinsically motivated.

FUELING EFFICACY

Self-efficacy is your understanding of your own ability to create positive results. If you have strong self-efficacy, you perceive yourself as capable and strong. It's a bit different from self-esteem, which is connected to appreciation or liking. Self-efficacy is about competence. Three points from research:

1. Self-efficacy grows from achievement, not visa versa. This means no matter how much you praise and encourage and tell a child he's fabulous... it won't create a sense of inner power. On the other hand, when he takes on a challenge and perseveres, he will feel a sense of efficacy. Efficacy grows from action.

2. The skills of emotional intelligence predict self-efficacy. Probably this correlation exists because emotionally intelligent children are more aware, intentional, and purposeful. They manage stress more effectively and motivate themselves to accomplish important goals. Emotional mastery leads to a sense of competence.

3. Self-efficacy predicts results. Children who recognize themselves as capable and responsible do a better job of exercising competence and responsibility. Thus building capacity is not just about capacity for that specific outcome. Helping the three-year-old make pancakes helps the six-year-old take new risks, which helps the 12-year-old take on big challenges.

Considering your own children, what is one example where you're building or have built capacity? What is one area where you'd like to do so? For example, for younger children, it might be brushing teeth, getting dressed, or cooking a dish like pancakes. For older kids, it could be building or making something interesting (rockets, stuffed animals, computers), working on homework without being reminded, or independently getting themselves ready for school.

Tools for Intrinsic Motivation

Try these approaches to help your child strengthen the fire within:

Build capacity. When you feel the need to do it for your kids, consider: *Is this an opportunity to build capacity so they have more strength later?*

Diminish product. When you are worried about how your child will do (e.g., on an assignment), remember that it's a learning opportunity, and making mistakes, trying again, and even failing are all essential parts of learning.

Adult in the child. Imagine your child in the future as a strong and capable adult. Use that image to help guide what you do now, for example, by providing opportunities to build capacity and letting her or him show competence.

SOME HOPE

It's a little funny reading back through this book now with a 16- and 14-year-old. Emma and Max just returned from two months in Vermont, and today while I write, Emma is on a 50-mile backpacking trip at her school. They are such competent, independent people that it's actually hard for me to remember the struggles of building capacity – the eggs on the floor, the tears in the laundry. In the midst of the struggle it feels infinite. It's not.

PRECIOUS FEELINGS (OR MAX'S NAP): WRAPPING UP PART II

When someone is experiencing a strong feeling, sometimes we try to help by saying, "It's not so bad." Imagine a child crying because she has to leave a friend's house. A typical reaction would be, "It's ok, sweetheart. You can see your friend again tomorrow." While that's very well intentioned, minimizing the negative experience to try to soothe your child may actually be sending a counterproductive message: *It's not ok to be sad.*

Sometimes when Max was a toddler and woke up from his naps, he was sad, especially when his mama wasn't home. Since Patty often used naptime for her work, and I was working at home, I struggled to keep wake-up time from being a descent into wailing. One day, I had an epiphany.

"I want Mama," sulked Max, which made me feel like he was accusing me of being the wrong parent.

My initial impulse was to react with hurt and say, "Well she's not here, and I am, so take or leave it, bub." I resisted, and instead said lovingly, "You really want Mama, don't you?"

"Yes," replied a slightly less vexed Max.

I forgot my plan for a moment and backslid saying, "I'm sorry she's not here, Maxie, but I'll snuggle with you." I was thinking, "She's going to be here in ten minutes, it's not that bad!" I suspect he sensed my effort to minimize his feelings.

"Go away, Daddy. I want *Mama*," re-escalated Max.

Again, part of me felt rejected. (Now I recognize that as one of my patterns.) Instead, I chose to notice the feeling Max was really expressing. I sat down on his little toddler bed and said, "I really miss her too. It's sad when she's not home."

"Yah," admitted Max, reaching out closer to me.

"She's such a good snuggler, and so warm and just right. I love her so much too – sometimes I really miss her."

"Yah," affirmed Max, now snuggling close to me.

"I wish we could both snuggle with her right now. She could hold you close, and we could all squeeze into your little bed. And we'd just have a lovely snuggle."

Suddenly, Max changed gears and spoke in his "you silly Daddy voice" saying, "But my bed isn't big enough."

When I tried to comfort Max by telling him the facts, I was forgetting (again) that facts are not relevant to the emotional brain. When I say, "You know Mama's going to be home soon, right?" I'm also implying, "You should not feel sad." While my intent may be kind, it's actually dismissive.

Max wanted his mama; facts wouldn't change that. When I stopped trying to "fix it" and participated in his world, he finally felt that I truly *understood* and could calm himself down.

The Power of Feeling Heard

It's fairly easy to see why it's important for a toddler to feel understood, but the premise is true for people of all ages. Feelings are real, even when the causes don't make sense to another person. And when people are sad, understanding is infinitely more caring that stating facts.

You can also validate your own emotions. When Hank, my stepdad, died, I was sad and angry. Despite the fact that I know anger is a normal part of grief, I found myself saying to myself, "You shouldn't be angry." It was when I could acknowledge my anger without judgment that it subsided.

It's another kind of Aikido. The basic premise of this martial art is to move out of the line of combat. Someone's running at you, you flow around him, shifting so you're at his side and you let his forward energy carry him away (and maybe flip him through the air for good measure).

When you try to directly combat or dismiss emotions like sadness or grief, you get bruised. When you shift so you're on the same side, you gain insight and acceptance. One way you can do this is with the VET process:

The VET Process

Validate = accept, honor, value the feelings

Explore = listen, question with curiosity, discover the messages of the feelings

Transform = move forward in a new way with new feelings

One of the biggest challenges with the VET process is that people, especially adults (and maybe extra especially dads), want to skip the first two steps (validate and explore) and jump right to the last step (transform). We try to fix the feeling.

Instead, try to first *learn from the feeling*, and then fix the real problem. If you're working hard to transform your feeling or your kid's, you have not done enough validating and exploring. The transforming will happen easily once you've listened to the feeling.

I've noticed that often I resist validating others' feelings. I had a Big Fight with Patty, and she was upset, and even more upset that I was not acknowledging that she was upset. But I thought she was wrong, and I thought that if I acknowledged her feelings, she would think that I agreed with her. That didn't work out so well.

I've noticed that parents often invalidate the child's feelings because they don't like a behavior. When my son had toddler meltdowns in the grocery store, the last thing I was inclined to do was sit down on at his eye level and validate his feelings. Yet over and over, I've found that's the fastest, most powerful way of salvaging the situation.

Validating someone's feelings is not the same as agreeing with that person's thoughts or actions. Validating feelings is recognizing, connecting, and honoring that what this person is experiencing emotionally is important.

In addition to helping you and your child navigate emotions, this process is at the core of empathy, which is one of the key skills in Part III.

PART III

Give Yourself

What if we could each see our own vision of the future more clearly and use that to inform our parenting?

In Part III

Introduction: Touching the Future

Chapter 7: From War to Peace

> **Increase empathy**: Tune into others' feelings and respond appropriately.

Chapter 8: Creating the Future

> **Pursue noble goals**: Connect with your deep sense of purpose to remember what's truly important.

Chapter 9: Helping Children Give Themselves

INTRODUCTION TO PART III:
Touching the Future

My stepdad, Hank, was a large presence in our family, for good and ill. He and my mom met when I was about three years old, and he was an incredible father figure. He took us backpacking, taught me to make and fly kites, to sail, to love nature. They were married when I was ten, and after about five years of a rollercoaster relationship (infidelity, conflict, resolution, lying, resolution, infidelity, more conflict, trial separation, etc.), they divorced when I was 17.

It took several years and many difficult conversations, but Hank and I eventually restored a close relationship. We saw each other often, he danced with Patty at our wedding, and he was our children's grandfather.

When Hank was in hospital dying from cancer, my brother and I started talking; there where things we'd always thought we'd have time to do or talk about with Hank, and suddenly we were running out of time. Then next day, I went to the hospital with a short list.

Hank had always been this huge presence in my life, 6 foot 3 inches, larger than life. A few weeks before he'd been climbing on the ladder putting lights on the giant Christmas tree in his living room. But lying there, he seemed so small and old, his hair wispy, his muscles slack. I said something like this:

> I don't want you to die, but I want you to know that it's ok if you need to. I know there is so much we all regret about the way things went with you and my mom, and we all had a lot of hurt from that. But at the same time, I want you to see that now we're all doing well – and you are part of that too. I look at Emma and Max, and I see so much of what I love about them has come from you. The way Emma likes to think about problems, and the way Max loves being in the woods, you gave those things to me, and in turn, to them. No matter what happens, you are part of our family.

I'd always thought it would be near impossible to forgive him after those years of his untrustworthy behavior. But in this conversation I did, and it was easy. I did not say the words, "I forgive you," but it was much the same. I was practicing *making others good*, a powerful process I'll explain in this part of the book.

It was as if the proverbial weight slipped off his shoulders. I thought I was doing it for him, but of course I shed a huge burden as well. In that moment, it was effortless. It was as simple as turning around and embracing the gifts of our relationship.

The other insight that's stuck with me from that day is about the future. Before this, I had a vague sense that parenthood ripples across time. In training EQ practitioners in the Six Seconds' network, I'd heard hundreds of stories of the wonderful and terrible legacies of parents or grandparents or even great grandparents playing out over the generations. But in this conversation with Hank, it was visceral for me: We are directly touching the future.

I've been a contractor and built houses that will last some time. I've been a teacher and influenced the adults children will become. I've helped create a global nonprofit organization that's transformed thousands of lives. But in that moment with Hank, I vividly saw that nothing else in my life has the kind of direct link between today and tomorrow that occurs in parenting. My choices today affect the future my children create in their lives, in their children's lives, in their communities, in our world.

This is an awesome realization, grave and joyful in equal measure. I think it's a major reason why parenthood is so scary.

At the very same time, as I look at my story of Angelica from Mexico and David, my dad (see page 81), I see that we are not our parents' choices, and they are not ours. Instead it's like waves on the shore. The waves shape the sand; the sand shapes the waves. They are two parts of one interlocked whole.

I wrote this part of the book in Luang Prabang – a small city in the tropical mountains of Laos. There is a bridge across the river flowing fast and brown some 50 feet below, the kids called it "the sketchy bridge" because of the rusted metal and half-rotted planks. It's an old bridge, now only for two-wheeled vehicles and walking. The first time we walked across, which was pretty terrifying. Then we decided to try riding our bikes.

Fortunately, on the "bike lane" you can't clearly see the plummet to the river below. I put "bike lane" in quotes because it's four planks wide. Then a couple feet to the left are four planks for traffic the other direction. At least there are rails.

During the week while I was writing there in the Laos mountains, every day to go to lunch and then to dinner we rode our bikes across the bridge, and I came to view it much like parenting. To cross the bridge, you need some courage. You need to pedal – to put in energy. And you need to stay balanced. If you overcorrect, you're stuffed. When there's a gust of wind and you get near the edge of the four-plank-wide-lane, the temptation is to swerve and overcorrect. This is Not a Good Idea on the bridge... or in parenting.

You also need to focus on the present and how it's moving toward the future. Looking behind for a moment is helpful (any motorcycles rushing up?), looking ahead is invaluable (yes, I am going to make it across), but the future is made by the present, one pedal at a time. As a parent, the future is made by the present, one interaction at a time.

In this part of the book, the goal is to consider the future and the Give Yourself step in the model. It's time to consider big questions: Why did you want to be a parent? What is the impact you want to have, the legacy you're creating? And most important, how do you check to see that the choices you're making today are moving in the direction you want to go? Chapter 7 will explore the competency *increase empathy*, and chapter 8 will explore *pursue noble goals*.

"

To cross the bridge, you need some courage. You need to pedal – to put in energy. And you need to stay balanced.

"

Chapter 7: From War to Peace

Empathy is the ability to create an emotional connection with others – an effort to feel what they feel. It requires tuning into others' feelings, and finding or creating a match within your own feelings. In the model, we call this competency *increase empathy*. We can choose to actively engage in empathy as we learn to Give Ourselves.

Sometimes it's easy to empathize with our kids. We feel tender and open, and compassion just flows. When they're annoying, however, it's a different story. They're caught up in a pattern, we're caught up in a pattern, and frustration escalates.

Emma, at age nine, frequently made a big fuss when it's time to do work that was not appealing, especially "dumb writing homework" (despite usually liking writing and being an outstanding student). This was not new, but one time I noticed myself becoming highly reactive. I was getting more and more irritated with her, and the irritation about homework seemed to be bleeding into our relationship in general.

I'd say hello in the morning, and she'd grouch at me. I'd say hello in the afternoon, and she'd ignore me. Then the homework fuss would come up, and I found myself judgmentally labeling her as *drama queen, irrational, mean*, and a few I won't put in print. As my frustration grew, I found myself thinking things like, *She can bloody well sit in her room until the work is done.* I was angry, and I wanted to punish her.

There are two aspects of this reaction that I'd like to explore with you:

First, when I felt disrespected and excluded, my patience for the homework drama plummeted. My hurt feelings translated to wanting to hurt back.

Second, as I was feeling impatient, I fell into a pattern of focusing on facts and using force. Even though I *know this does not work*.

PARADIGM OF FACTS, FORCE, OR FEAR

In Six Seconds' work on change, we teach that people behave the way they do for emotionally valid reasons. As a result, unless you change the emotional dynamic underlying your behavior, you won't change. Alan Deutschman explains this concept well in *Change or Die*. (Deutschman's work influenced me to write the book *Inside Change* with Max Ghini.) Deutschman says the dominant, but failing, paradigm when trying to drive change is to use *facts, force,* and *fear*.

For example:

Facts: "Emma, You did this wrong. You're supposed write two pages, and you wrote only one."

Force: "You have to write another page right now, damn it!"

Fear: "If you don't do this correctly, you don't event want to know what's going to happen."

In hindsight, I was stuck in my pattern: As I got more frustrated, I began to rely on power and control. I started using facts to back up how right I was, force to reinforce my sense of power, and fear to accentuate my own power over her.

In the facts–force–fear paradigm, we try to *make* people change. This doesn't work, because people don't want to be forced. When people feel pushed, they resist. Then they start to self-protect, dig in their heels, and become less open to risk doing something different. Meanwhile as we push, we become more irritated and less open to understand what they're feeling and what's really blocking the change.

Nice mess. I *know* this, but knowledge is not enough. There I was getting frustrated with my daughter, and the more frustrated I got, the more I found myself barreling down this wrong track, a track that I intellectually knew leads only to more frustration. But nonetheless, I was sucked in. And the more irritated I got, the more distance I created, accelerating this reactive, superficial, destructive mindset.

Once I started to reflect, I could see the costs of the pattern. Recognizing the emotional dynamic is only the first step. Changing my behavior required a shift in thinking and emotions.

Fortunately, it came one evening at bedtime.

I was kissing Emma goodnight, and she had a rare evening with no book in hand and welcomed a sleepy snuggle. She seemed so big and so fierce in her opinions. But laying next to her that night, I had this vivid memory of our first long plane ride and told her about it.

She was under six months old. We were flying from San Francisco to London. As long as one of us was walking around holding her, Emma was content. But as soon as we sat down, she fussed. I remember walking up and down the long 747 aisles in the dark, with glimpses of snowy Greenland at night as we walked past the rows of windows, pacing endlessly at 500 miles per hour with this sleepy warm angel.

I remember quietly singing the same little song over and over and over (*la mar estaba serena, serena estaba la mar...* the sea was calm, calm was the sea). Probably as much for me as her. I can still feel the soothing rhythm of it.

I remember looking out the small galley window, watching the endless stretches of Nordic ice in the moonlight and wondering at the infinite variety of that unknown alien landscape, so cold and distant.

At the time, I had no sense that this would become a precious memory, but now it's so vivid and tinged with the sepia tones of nostalgia. Amazing what becomes printed in our hearts.

From that place of appreciation, the whole homework drama frustration simply evaporated. I remembered the precious (and willful) innocence inside this person. I *made her good* in my mind and heart and this let me stop being reactive about homework. This emotional connection is empathy, and it's a doorway to a whole new way of seeing – and the antidote to the facts–force–fear paradigm.

In the week following that evening, we didn't talk about changing the homework drama, it just didn't come up. It's like the circuit was diffused, at least for the moment, and I became more keenly aware of the trap – and at least one way out.

"

The first rule of emotional intelligence:
When people feel pushed, they resist.

"

In the Give Yourself part of the model, there are two key skills: *increase empathy* and *pursue noble goals.* The story above illustrates how these work together. As we build empathy, it unlocks the possibility of responding in a totally new way – a way aligned with our highest goals.

So how do we actually make this shift and open the door of empathy? It turns out, it's not just about action.

Don't Just Do Something

Empathy is the ability to create a meaningful emotional connection with another person. It doesn't mean solving a problem. It doesn't mean answering. It means being fully present and creating a space where you and the other person can meet.

I remember one time when Max was a toddler, I took him to get a birthday present for Patty. We drove over the mountain to Los Gatos to Sur la Table, a wonderful cooking shop. I was excited about the outing, both getting Patty a present I knew she'd like and having "daddy time" with Max. He was not super excited and fell asleep in the car.

We arrived in the parking lot, he woke up and I enthusiastically said, "Let's go!" He did not want to. I coaxed and persuaded and scolded and pushed, and finally bodily picked him up. I'm carrying a screaming boy to go do something fun. Oops.

I returned to the parking lot, put him back in his seat, apologized, sat in the car, put on some music, and waited. After about two minutes, I said, "You're feeling pretty tired, aren't you?" "Yah," said Max. After about two more minutes, I said, "Do you want to go get a smoothie and Mama's present?" "Ok," said Max.

I was reminded of a line from David Tubley, one of Six Seconds' regional network directors. One of David's favorite lines is a play on the "normal" phrase, "Don't just sit there, do something." When it comes to increasing empathy, David's advice: *Don't just* do *something,* sit there. When we get too focused on solving and fixing and pushing, we don't leave space for empathy.

It's extremely difficult to feel empathy when you're tapped out, though.

On days when we're overtired, overstressed, and barely able to find time to pee much less eat, there won't be a lot of bandwidth left for empathy.

One key tool for increasing empathy with your kids is creating moments where you connect with simple pleasures. This can happen serendipitously, especially if stay alert, but you can also make it happen.

THE GOOD LIFE OF *SOPA DE LIMA*

One summer evening I worked in the garden with the kids and then we enjoyed a build-your-own-soup party. It was one of those evenings that reminds us of the good life – the life worth appreciating and living fully.

The evening began with Max and me in the garden, shoveling topsoil from the pickup truck. Max, just shy of three feet tall, stood in the back of the truck with his tiny shovel. "I am a tractor," said Max, jumping on the dirt and pushing it around. "Heaaaavy," he said, and flung more onto the driveway.

"Let's scoop the dirt into the bucket, Max," I said. "Oh-kay," sang Max.

In addition to the pleasure of watching Max's abundant joy, I loved the smell of the warm, fertile soil; the easy rhythm of shovels filling the bucket; the healthy color of the dark earth in the garden.

After getting thoroughly dirty, we went inside to wash up. Neither Patty or I had thought about dinner, but we happened to have a nice assortment of tomatoes, avocados, and leftover chicken – just the right start for *sopa de lima*, a kind of tortilla soup (recipe to follow).

After a few minutes of cutting up ingredients, Patty and I attempted to move everyone to the table. Small pause for tantrums (Max wanted more apricots, Emma wanted more movie), and dinner began.

Emma had not had *sopa de lima* in her conscious memory, and so she was somewhat recalcitrant. "I don't like corn."

"You liked it last night."

"But that was on the – it was big. This is little. I like big corn."

"Oh. Well, I see. This is big corn. I just cut it off the cob – would you try a tiny taste?"

Soon Emma got into the spirit of dinner. She was a child who narrated her world. It was like a soundtrack: "Oh, it's a buffet! Buffets are my favorite, and there is no paying for this buffet. How come it doesn't take money for this buffet? Mix, mix, need more corn! Oh, add some chips. Yummy!"

Meanwhile, Max was onto his second bowl. Silence from the high chair meant dinner is just right!

My bowl of *sopa de lima* that night was bursting with ruby red tomato, creamy avocado, tingly salsa, and (of course) fresh lime juice – a complex yet simple mix of ingredients, just like so many good times to be cherished as a parent.

It is enjoying simple pleasures, like shoveling dirt and having a bowl of soup, that we become more present, practice gratitude, and recharge ourselves so we can have the emotional energy and wellbeing that helps us feel empathy.

Make-Your-Own *Sopa de Lima* á la Freedman Family

- Around 1 quart of chicken broth
- 2–3 ears of corn
- Olive oil for the pan
- 1 ripe avocado (Max would suggest 2)
- 1 vine-ripe red tomato
- Leftover chicken
- Green onion
- Cilantro

- 2–3 limes

- Monterey Jack cheese

- Leftover rice, optional

- Hot sauce or salsa, to taste

- Corn chips or corn tortillas

- Salt and pepper, to taste

Of course, these are rough guidelines. You can substitute almost any-thing on the list. Remember, this is for a meal when you were too busy playing in the garden to plan dinner.

The soup takes about ten minutes to prepare if you have two people slicing. Start by putting the broth in a pot over high heat. By the time it boils, you'll be done prepping the buffet of other ingredients.

Slice the corn off the cob and sauté in olive oil for about five minutes over high heat; add salt and pepper to taste. When the corn is tender, put it in a small bowl on the table.

Cube the avocado, tomato, and chicken. Dice the green onion. Rough chop the cilantro. Quarter the limes. Shred some cheese. Put each in-gredient in a separate bowl on the table.

Put rice, chips, tortillas, or salsa in bowls on the table, along with the hot sauce. Bring the pot of hot broth to the table with a ladle.

Each person puts whatever items she wants in her bowl, and then you ladle hot broth over the top. Sprinkle broken corn chips or torn tortillas on top.

The most important ingredient in this *sopa de lima* is appreciation. Notice the good life. Let it fill you up. Then, from that abundance, can you find a deeper level of empathy?

The real secret of the recipe is simple abundance, the flavors of love, the feeling of choice, and the joy of experimenting, of discovering something new together.

Suspend and Attend

Mimi Frenette, a member of Six Seconds' network of emotional intelligence practitioners, suggested the trick to empathy is to *suspend and attend*. Suspend judgment. Stop getting ready with your reply. Put aside your impulse to solve or fix. Then attend to what's really happening with the other person. Not just the obvious, but what's underneath.

In the "War to Peace" and "*Sopa de Lima*" stories, I focused on appreciation as a doorway to empathy. Curiosity is another powerful tool. Both of these feelings shift our focus to others and help us tune in.

 Genuine curiosity brings me on a quest to understand someone else's perspective. Appreciation makes me want to do so. If my son is resisting doing homework and I start wondering, *I wonder what's driving his reaction?*, then my curiosity helps me see a new perspective. If I can connect with my love and appreciation for him (rather than my frustration or fear), then I feel committed to taking this step.

Empathy, in itself, can be transformational. We can make it even more powerful by linking empathy to larger goal, to our core vision. If you can see where you *really* want to go, and then bring empathy into action, you're able to go in a powerful direction and bring others, including your kids, along with you. The next step is clarifying your vision of the future – for your kids, and for yourself.

The real secret of the recipe is simple abundance, the flavors of love, the feeling of choice, and the joy of experimenting, of discovering something new together.

Chapter 8: Choosing the Future – Pursue Noble Goals

One of Emma's observations, at age six: "If Maxie says something mean to me, and I say something mean to Maxie, then we might forget how to forgive."

I was sitting with Max and Emma and reading them an article by meditation leader Christine Easwaran about being kind. I read a sentence and then asked them what it meant (search for "Easwaran" on 6seconds.org if you want to try this).

One message of the article is that we can each contribute to world peace by being kind. I often ask the kids, "What are you adding to the world right now?" Or when they were little, "Are you making the world a friendlier place, or a 'fightier' place?"

As we explore the competency *pursue noble goals*, ask yourself: *What did you add to the world today? Is that the contribution you most want to make?*

What's really important?

The kids ate ice pops, and we talked about lofty ideals (in the language of four- and six-year-olds). I asked Emma and Max (separately), "What is important in our family?"

Max's replies: not to fight, to be kind to each other, to help each other when we get hurt, to say "hi" to people when we don't know them and ask their names, that you (Daddy) go to work and help people.

I asked, "What about rocks?" (Max's obsession from ages three to seven). "No, rocks are important to me, but not to the whole family."

Emma's replies: not hitting, using kind words, cleaning up after yourself instead of making other people clean up after you, being healthy, being safe and staying near a grownup, telling the truth.

Their choices were fascinating to me. It told me some of our efforts were sinking in, and that there are areas where we needed to be more articulate and explicit. For example, I would have thought, love would be near the top of the list, so maybe we should talk more about that.

What are the important things in your family, in your company or school, and in your life? Do you invest time in them? Do your children see and hear you putting those priorities into action?

Christine's husband, renowned meditation leader Eknath Easwaran, wrote, "By our choices, each of us helps to shape the destiny of us all." The collective effects of our choices are clear in our families, and increasingly clear in the world as a whole. What we do and how we do it affects many, many people. So starting with ourselves, and then our families, then our teams and organizations and communities – what kind of world are we choosing to create?

This is at the heart of *pursuing noble goals*. Your noble goal is your answer to the question: What are you choosing to create? It's about your vision of who you want to be, including in your role as a parent, about what you want to add to the world. This vision is about a better future – for ourselves individually, our children, families, friends, workplaces, schools, and communities.

Children often talk about "what I want to be when I grow up." This kind of future thinking is invaluable for kids – and for adults. As we explore and clarify our future vision, it creates motivation to take steps in the present.

WHEN I GROW BIGGER BIGGER

On a walk with Emma when she was a toddler: "Daddy, when I grow bigger bigger, I want to be a firefighter," she piped, in her small high voice.

Emma spoke carefully, each word equally articulated, and with the total certainty of someone who has passed the wise age of two-and-a-half years.

After a moment, she turned to me. "Daddy, when you get bigger bigger, what do you want to be?"

I asked Emma, "What do you think I am going to be?"

"When you grow up, you will be an elephant," she answered.

"What about me?" asked Patty.

"You can be an elephant too."

"That's good," Patty told me squeezing my hand. "We can be elephants together."

I love the idea of being an elephant. Powerful. Gentle. Playful. Wise. Affectionate.

I want more of those qualities in my life. When I get "bigger bigger" I want to be clear. I want to be patient. I want to have a plan but also be flexible.

When I get bigger bigger, I want to see the difference between a seductive fiction and a meaningful intention. I want to be guided by both my heart and mind, so I can seek out wisdom. I want to balance the future with the present.

Who do you want to be when you get "bigger bigger"?

What do you want for your child?

Parents' most frequent answer to this question for their children, by far, is "happiness." I think that word has become shorthand for a whole collection of ingredients that doesn't give us a lot of guidance as parents. If we want our children to be happy in the future, does it mean we let them do whatever they want now, so life is easy and pleasant? Does it mean we discipline them harshly, so they will be obedient and follow the path we've planned?

The challenge I see is that I meet parents in California, India, Africa, Japan, Australia, and everywhere in between, and many say they want their children to be happy, but they mean very different things. Some want the child to go to the best university in the country. Some want the child to have a "good job." Some want the child to feel totally special. Some want the child to meaningfully contribute

Just as a long-term vision is powerful for us, it's invaluable for our children. A sense of vision and purpose for a four-year-old might be very simple. We helped Max think about being an "earth hero" when he was a toddler, and used this as a reminder to not hurt plants, leave trash, etc. Over the years, it's evolved for both kids into a deeper motivation.

ORANGUTAN HEART

Many years after that "bigger bigger" walk, we were preparing for our first visit to Borneo, the largest island in Asia. Max, now eight, saw a video on YouTube that talked about orangutans being endangered by deforestation, and both kids became quite concerned. Max picked this topic as his school project, so we arranged our trip to spend several days where we could see and learn about these fascinating creatures.

As we traveled, the kids were asking questions and making comments about the destruction of rainforest for creation of palm-oil plantations. Max was inclined to blame the Malaysian people for this problem. We talked about the sad reality that we've made similar environmental tradeoffs for commerce in our country, as has virtually every country around the globe. We can be sad, angry, or some combination about the situation, but we need to do so without putting ourselves above anyone else. In this discussion, Max began to tear up – and talked about how sad he felt about the plight of the orangutans.

At our last visit to Sepilok Rehabilitation Center, Emma interviewed one of the scientists. At the end, Emma asked what she could do to help. Thankfully, this scientist didn't do the usual adult "these are grownup problems" dismissal. Instead, she told Emma that the center needs to raise awareness and funds, and kids can do that too.

As we left, the four of us continued to discuss this challenge. Something clicked. The kids began thinking of more and more ways they could help. It as if all their frustration, fear, and sorrow for the orangutans suddenly funneled into concern, passion, and commitment to do something about their plight.

In the taxi on the way home from dinner, Patty suggested that the kids have had a lot of success asking for support from family and friends for projects like readathons. I suggested that we could invent a new "athon" – a postcard-athon – and get sponsorships for sending postcards that would raise awareness. The kids took the idea and ran. Ideas were flying. Finally I said they had to wait to share new ideas until we got back to our room, so I could take notes for them. They were hopping up and down trying to hold onto their ideas.

Back at the hotel, they talked *nonstop* for hours, and we were having a seriously hard time getting them to go to sleep. They were vibrating with passion and hope. Maxie said, "I really want to help." My answer: "That's good, because they need you."

In the Six Seconds Model, the capstone is a competency we call *pursue noble goals*. Our view is that when one takes a commitment to a larger purpose, it unlocks a new level of emotional power. There is an incredible feeling that grows from taking action – small actions and big ones – that serves something larger. This connection becomes a catalyst that transforms emotions at a profound level: in Max and Emma's case, from sorrow and anger into a fiercely joyful passion. Knowing that you can make a difference sparks some essential human capacity and awakens the unstoppable energy that has fueled every positive change in the human experience.

Laying in bed, Emma and Max were whispering to each other about how much of their own savings they're willing to invest in funding their action project. Maxie whispered to her, "I can't believe this is really happening. I've always wanted to do something like this."

We finally got them settled down, Emma writing and Max furiously thinking. Emma insisted on reading us one more plan, which we all liked. I fiercely told them it was *really* time to sleep. After a moment of silence, Emma said, "Daddy, one more thing."

"Ok, sweetheart, just *one* more."

"Thank you for taking us seriously."

That little comment rocked me. How often have I missed a chance to see my children, all children, as capable, powerful people? How much better could their lives and the world be if we took children's aspirations seriously?

When we feel that sense of *I can contribute to the world,* it unlocks something in us. In the following years, Emma raised money for the orangutans. She used her own money to pay to go back to Borneo to conduct an analysis of water quality in the Kinabatangan River. She made numerous presentations to school kids on our travels and raised more money for the rainforest. The sense of purpose catalyzed a commitment to do the hard work.

The emotional effect was profound. Here was a child who was cautious, perfectionistic, and introverted. Now she's given talks all around the world. Why? One time she said: "The orangutans can't talk, so I have to talk for them." Her sense of purpose pushed and pulled her to go beyond what's comfortable – to change her patterns, to be a stronger version of herself.

DEFINING YOUR NOBLE GOAL

A *noble goal* is a short, compelling statement of purpose. Typically we phrase it with a verb, which gives you an idea of your approach, and then a statement of what we want to add in the world. Mine is: *To inspire compassionate wisdom.*

For me, it's a reminder about why I do my work, but it's also a reminder about who I want to be as a father, a husband, a friend, really every role in my life. I chose the verb *inspire* because I want to add energy and possibility. I chose *compassionate wisdom* as a reminder to myself not to get caught in the pattern of being right – of focusing on the surface facts instead of what's important.

If you decide you want to develop or clarify yours, here are five criteria we use to define a noble goal:

Outer directed: A noble goal will help you, but the focus is on others. What do you want to add to the world? This helps move out of that "self above others" reaction process.

Beyond your lifetime: A noble goal isn't something you complete (such as "clean up this river"), it's enduring (such as, "support people to live in harmony with nature"). This helps build a long-term focus.

Integrating all domains: A noble goal is something you can serve at work, at home, in the community, by yourself, with others, in every domain in your life. It's not just about your work or your family; it's about your whole life. This allows you to make it part of your daily life.

Energizing: As in the story about Emma and the orangutans, your noble goal needs to spark the fire within. It gives you energy to face challenges and be your best.

Collaborative: To qualify as a noble goal, it needs to be something that does not diminish others. When you pursue noble goals, you sustain and support others to identify and pursue theirs. This helps you stay out of ego and power struggles – and makes you a much more powerful parent.

One way of crafting your noble goal is to consider your legacy. Imagine that your children have children who have children, and after you're no longer around to play with the grandchildren, there is a big family reunion. They start talking about how the world is getting to be a better place, and someone mentions your name. Your grandchild, or great-grandchild, has been affected by your legacy, and she talks about how you were part of making the family and the world better. *What do you want her to say about you?*

Using Your Noble Goal

Once you've created that short, compelling statement of purpose, the next step is to *pursue* it, to live it. Your noble goal won't be complete in your lifetime. It's not something to do or chase. It's something to be.

Your noble goal is a reminder of who you want to be today. Who you want to be when it's a fun day at the park, who you want to be when you're in the epic battle of getting out the door in the morning. Perhaps especially in these moments of challenge, ask yourself: *Am I living my noble goal right now?* If not, *carpe diem.* The next moment is another chance to try again.

As parents, there is so much in each day – so many moments, challenges, demands. And so much to see and learn and explore – if we choose to be awake. Yet tomorrow is not far away and the day those great-grandchildren are talking about you is just a blink away.

Your noble goal won't be complete in your lifetime. It's not something to do or chase. It's something to be.

Chapter 9:
Teaching About Give Yourself

Just as with Know Yourself and Choose Yourself, the most powerful way to teach the Give Yourself part of the model is to practice it. When you do, you will automatically be teaching it to your kids because you will not react in the same old ways. And when you change your end of the pattern, the kids will find there's an opportunity for them to do the same.

Here are some milestones to work toward at various ages:

Self-Direction Goals

Ages 0-4: Notice that other people have feelings, and your choices affect how others feel. Learn to notice that you affect other people around you, and other people affect you.

Ages 5-7: Learn that your choices have an effect on the larger world, which means you make a difference. Practice being intentionally kind and generous, even when it's difficult.

Ages 8-11: Learn to empathize with others, even when you disagree. Begin dreaming about the present and future you want to live in. You can already do something at school, with friends, at sports.

Ages 12-15: Notice the world and people around you and your role in it. What do you want to improve or change? Where and how can you contribute? Who could you call onboard with you to share your ideas? Who could support and guide you? How can you build caring relationships to do so?

Ages 16+: Feel confident that you have power, and therefore, responsibility to affect the world in positive ways. Since you're not alone in doing that, connect and collaborate with others to share your goals and act coherently. Know you are part of an interconnected fabric of life; feel you have both responsibility and benefit from this connection.

Tools for Empathy

Try these techniques to help practice empathy:

Reasonable emotions. If you're in a stress reaction and your kid is in a stress reaction, your communication will not be peaceful – and you won't get the real story. To understand the range of emotions at play, including the emotions hidden under other emotions, you need to add some peace and compassion to the equation. Once you begin to see that the emotions at play are there for a reason and that they're reasonable, you're on the road to understanding them.

It's not about me. Your child's reactions may have little or nothing to do with you. Consider: Maybe he's not provoking or resisting *you*, maybe he's having a challenge with himself or someone else.

Pause for curiosity. When your child is reacting in a way that's triggering your reactions, pause and ask yourself: *I wonder what's going on for him?*

A WISH FOR EMPATHY

When Max was 13, I was unhappy about his lack of homework progress and said: "I've told you a thousand times, just do your #$@**@ work and we can stop fighting. Why don't you just listen to me???? I hate having to shout to get you to pay attention."

Yes, I realize that's not a very effective way to communicate.

Yes, I'm supposed to be an "expert" on emotional intelligence.

Yes, you're right; there's a total lack of empathy getting in the way.

We recently surveyed several hundred parents about their biggest challenges, and the key emotional intelligence (EQ) skills every parent needs. I found that I'm not alone in this kind of communication train wreck. The most frequent issue parents said they want to improve: peaceful communication.

Creating a collaborative, peaceful relationship with our children is a huge test of emotional intelligence – and particularly empathy. In the example of my "noncommunication" with my son about homework, there are a number of emotional intelligence failures:

I escalated, so I was reacting unconsciously instead of responding intentionally. Underneath my anger was a feeling of powerlessness and fear. I was scared that he is not self-motivated and won't do well. I reacted to the fear by attacking.

I was trying to use my force of will to "make" him comply. The first rule of emotional intelligence: *When people feel pushed, they resist.*

I was blaming him, interpreting his lack of interest in homework as a kind of personal attack on me. I blamed him, saying that he was making me behave the way that I behaved.

I was focused on what I wanted and my perspective. I was certain that I was right, and therefore he was wrong.

Tools for Giving Yourself

Here are three techniques to practice for giving time:

Schedule time to give. Consciously set aside some time as a gift for your child. Put it in your calendar. Communicate with your child so she or he knows how much time you've made available. Let it be the child's choice of what to do; you've given it freely.

Give back. Just as you are giving time to your child, look for opportunities to help your child give time to others. You can encourage him or her, for example, "I would appreciate it if you'd sit with me for a minute while I'm relaxing on the couch."

Word match. Just as with *take* and *give*, there are many words we use (out loud or in our own heads) that have an emotional connotation. What's the emotional message you want to send? Use words that match.

I'd like to focus on this last point, because it turns out that this lack of perspective-taking – this lack of empathy – is the key to unraveling much parent–child tension. In the cool light of self-reflection, I can now look back at the exchange and realize that my sense of righteous anger was blocking me from advancing the conversation.

When I increase empathy and relook at the situation with compassion, I see a different story. Perhaps he was afraid, too. Perhaps he felt powerless, too. Perhaps he's learned the exact same pattern I've modeled: When you're afraid, attack. Perhaps our power struggle was simply two people afraid to honestly share their fears.

Of course, writing this is painful. This isn't the kind of father I want to be. The good news is that I'm certain this same pattern will arise again this week. We'll have a chance, probably many chances, to retry this interaction. Hopefully, tomorrow I'll remember to take that all-important pause and ask myself: *I wonder what's really going on for him right now?*

That moment of curiosity is the doorway to empathy, and it's a game changer. Empathy is not actually a complex skill. As we know from neuroscientists like Marco Iacoboni (search for him on 6seconds.org), we're wired for empathy – it's a basic part of the social brain. However, as stress increases, it's harder for us to access empathy. That little pause of curiosity is a way to step out of the stress reaction, and step into being the person we choose to be.

GIVING TIME

Language is intriguing. Will you *take time* to listen to your child today? Or will you *give time* to listen to your child today? What's the difference?

Karen McCown, Six Seconds' founder, often points out this distinction. When we take time, our focus is on self. It's like saying, *I'm really busy, but I'm going to sacrifice what I want to help you.* When we give time, it's a gift.

This is quite helpful with young children who like to endlessly do boring things. I'm sorry, but there it is: What's interesting to a toddler just doesn't engage my interest for long. When Emma was a toddler, she and I played a game where I'd stack blocks and knock them down. We had a little hand puppet beaver, and beaver was a little naughty. Daddy would stack the blocks, and beaver would knock them down. Many, many times.

I did not play this game because it was fun for me. I played it because it was fun for her, and that delighted me (and sometimes beaver would chomp on her toes and she'd giggle). I chose to give her the time, and once I'd made that decision, it really didn't matter to me what we did — it was her time. It was a gift for her to do with as she pleased.

This is also challenging as kids get older. I'm working, and Max comes into the office with a question or even just to tell me that dinnertime is coming soon. I have a choice: Do I take time away from my work, or do I stop working and give him time because he's important? I'm sorry to say that I often fail to seize these opportunities.

One way to help make this decision is to consider your values. Here's an activity to help you do so:

Vision Alignment Activity

First, ask yourself: What are some of the qualities, characteristics, and achievements that you consider essential for your child to have? Make a list of 10–15 items. Here are some examples — you can use these, and/or add your own. It may be difficult to choose only 10–15.

- Self-awareness
- Vision / passion / direction in life
- Inner peace
- Self-respect
- Self-care / balance
- Physical health / strength / energy
- Kindness/caring toward others
- Respect toward others

- Dutiful / obedient / follow rules
- Ethical / moral
- Religious / spiritual
- Creative / inventive / expressive
- Good manners / etiquette
- Contribute to the world / to others
- Strong personal relationships
- Good looks / fashion sense / grooming
- Networking / form connections
- To love you
- To value family
- To respect you / to fear you
- Positive relationships with teachers
- Love learning
- Earn high test scores / grades
- Go to the best university
- High-paying / high-status job
- Job security
- Good job
- Important profession
- Be a good spouse
- Be a good parent... Be a good grandparent
- _____
- _____
- _____

Next, look carefully at your list. Are some of the items mutually exclusive? For example, I met a mother who wanted her son to *have a voice* and so encouraged him to speak his mind. Then when he was speaking up frequently, and very disrespectfully, she was surprised, saying: *but being respectful is one of our family's core values*. You can see how these two goals *voice* and *respect* could easily conflict, depending on how you taught them.

Tools for Defining Your Family's Values

To help clarify the values you want to teach your child, try these three strategies:

Prioritize values. Consider where you want to invest your time and resources. Identify any values that conflict. Decide which is the priority.

Align together. Check to see if your values match the values of other adults in your child's life. Where there are a gap or disagreement, there's an opportunity for an important conversation before the child becomes confused by the conflicting messages.

Translate values. When this value is coming to life, what does it look like or sound like? Now, consider how to express that based on your child's age. For example, if you value the environment, and your child is three, you might talk about being an Earth-protector.

Where you see a potential conflict, it's important to reflect and prioritize. If you have to choose between these two items, which do you choose? Is there a way to balance them?

To continue that line of exploration, the next step may be even harder: Take your list and rank the items. It's a forced ranking, meaning no ties. Within the top three, are there conflicts? Are you clear about which is most important?

Now, the "fun" part: Encourage your partner and other caregivers in your child's life to do this exercise. Are you all in agreement on the top priorities? Are there points of misalignment, even conflict? If you don't find a balance, compromise, or come to agreement, it's unlikely that your child will successfully integrate these conflicting priorities.

THE ROAD TO SUCCESS

One important consideration as you reflect on your goals for your child is the timeline. Where is success? This week? This year? This decade? 18 years old, 30, 60?

There is a fascinating project called the *Grant Study*. Starting in the late 1930s, the study tracked 268 men from Harvard University. By many people's reckoning, these men were already "successful"; after all, they were reasonably affluent, privileged – and all at Harvard! But the study asked, "What happens next?" For example, what will make some of these people successful or not?

If you go to 6seconds.org and search for "Grant Study," you'll see a couple of pieces sharing more about the study and comments made by George Valliant, the study's director for some 40 years. Valliant made two points that are powerful for me. The first is that we need focus on the long game – our job as parents isn't about this year or even this decade, it's about who our children will be in 30, 50, even 70 years:

> You cannot tell success at any given point – to understand success, you need to look at the arc of these men's lives, the long story.

Tools for Purpose

To strengthen your sense of purpose in your parenting, keep these three points in mind:

Relationships matter. If relationships are, indeed, the only thing that matters in the end, we can use this as a benchmark for all decisions. *Is this choice strengthening relationship with your child?*

Parent for the future. When you're evaluating a situation, consider what's important in this today – and what will be important in 5, 10, 20 years. Let the long-term guide your response.

Match up the what, how, and why. When you're caught up in what you're doing and how you're doing it, you might forget why you're doing what you do. Talk about that. Think about the future and evaluate: Are my choices today creating the future I want?

As we consider what we want for our children in their future, I encourage you to have both a long lens and a short lens. The long lens helps you see your vision for them in as adults. The short lens is about what it happening this week. What are you teaching, what are you building today?

Valliant's second point reminds me about the kind of relationship I want to create with my children, and the importance of their skills to build relationships with others:

> "In the end," Valliant said, "the only thing that really matters in life is your relationships to other people."

As I wrote in Part II about *building capacity* (page 137), the choices we're making today can be for the present only or for the long haul. This is not easy. My son and I were working on building some shelves, I was feeling impatient and thinking, "It would be faster to just this myself." But then I remembered about building capacity – and considered that it's not just the technical skills he has to build, but there's another question. How does he feel about the experience? My frustration was teaching him that this process was negative. I was undermining my own goal. If I want him to learn the skill and want to use it, I need to refocus and change the experience.

As you look with the two lenses, can you see places where today's choices are, in fact, building the future you want? On the other hand, are undermining your goals in some ways? If you hold onto the long view, does it help you shift your thinking about the interactions today?

This is why, in thinking about goals, it's useful to distinguish between the what, why, and how.

What is the outcome. Where will your child go?

How is the method. What path will your child follow?

Why is the driving force. Does your child actually want to go there?

The why creates the enduring power and makes the goal transformational. I suspect we get caught up in what and how and shortchange the why. As parents, we can easily get caught up in *doing the work*, but we may not pay enough attention to where we want that work to go.

Tools for Compassionate Conflict

To help your child solve interpersonal challenges, here are three techniques:

Create context. Sometimes a child feels overwhelmed because she perceives that no one else going through what she's going through, that she is the only one facing these challenges. When we ask our kids questions and share stories of others' challenges, it can help them see that they're not alone in a struggle – and that there are solutions.

Make others good. This is a reminder to engage with our children in a way that is compassionate, not just to our child, but to all. When your child faces a challenge, don't polarize. Don't see one person as the enemy – see, and help your child see, that we're in this together.

Help your child find a middle ground. In a disagreement, we can fight, or we can avoid. What other options are there?

FOURTH-GRADE *SATYAGRAHA*

Fourth grade was a fabulous year for Emma, with huge leaps of passion and learning and adventure. And powerful challenges. The most pressing was an ongoing conflict with another girl, let's call her Josie. They are both strong willed, independent, and smart. Patty and I had worked to help Emma see that *being right* is not that interesting unless you are also kind. In turn, Emma has worked hard on being less abrasive, but these two girls just pushed one another's buttons. Halfway through the year, it seemed like nearly every day Josie was accusing Emma of something.

In one incident, Josie was mad that Emma ignored her. "I don't want to fight with her, so I just walk away," said Emma. We all agreed that's better than fighting but not the same as making peace. Emma was at a loss, though, of how to engage in a different way and was feeling helpless. "She's mad at me no matter what I do," she said.

I shared a bit of Gandhi's story. Emma could definitely relate to the struggle against oppression, and found the concept of *satyagraha* fascinating. Satyagraha is the name Gandhi gave to the type of nonviolent resistance he led to transform India. Gandhi wrote:

> Truth (*satya*) implies love, and firmness (*agraha*) engenders and therefore serves as a synonym for force. I thus began to call the Indian movement *Satyagraha*, that is to say, the Force which is born of Truth and Love or non-violence.

He said satyagraha isn't passive resistance – that's like Emma choosing to walk away or ignore Josie. Satyagraha is active, it's a force, but it's not the kind of force most of us in the West think of when we think of "power." Yet it turns out to be a game-changing, world-changing power because it steps out of the paradigm of escalating might and righteousness. Satyagraha requires an acceptance of the other, seeing them not as an enemy, but as another part of the challenge you are in yourself. In other words, Emma and Josie are in this struggle together.

In this outlook, it's not just *what* you do that matters. *How* and *why* are just as important. For Gandhi, the means is the result – if you pursue peace through violence, you make violence. If you create peace through love, then you create love.

In fourth-grade terms, this means finding kindness and compassion for Josie, even if Emma doesn't like Josie's behavior. It means not ignoring, not walking away, but also not giving in or giving up. It meant Emma finding a way to respectfully say, "I'm going to do this by myself" without Josie hearing it as criticism or rejection. This required Emma to also feel respect for Josie.

Emma came back the next day having tried it. "Satyagraha is *so* difficult," she said, "but I am going to keep doing it." While she struggled with this practice, she also experienced in just one day that this is a transformational way of engaging with disagreement. In her description of the day, we could that she had, in fact, found a new kind of force.

As Gandhi said, when you let go of "violence of the heart," it generates a powerful new energy:

> What I have pleaded for is renunciation of violence of the heart – and consequent active exercise of the force generated by the great renunciation.

The challenge is maintaining it – holding onto kindness in the midst of daily frustrations. While Emma could choose her response, Josie continued to look for opportunities to blame. It felt impossible for Emma, as a nine-year-old, not take this personally. It's difficult even for adults to step back and not take someone else's reactivity personally.

The solution comes back to *making others good*. It means letting go of being right over kindness. It means accepting, "She is doing her best, and I could do no better if I were her." The challenge: While our egos are saying, *She's mean and bad*, how can we make her good? We need to find something to care about so we can let go of being more-right-than-the-other-person.

Satyagraha is a process of resistance and a force of power, and an exercise in justice. At the core, it is change that starts with love.

LET THEM LEAD

In the story about orangutans, Emma saying, "Thank you for taking us seriously," leads to a piece of advice that applies equally to helping children develop intrinsic motivation and pursue their own noble goals. *Find ways for them to be in charge.*

Max, as the youngest in the family, has spent much of his life being directed by others. Unfortunately, he's developed a pattern around this, where he assumes that others are trying to control him – and *when people feel pushed, they resist.* This combination has led to a lot of conflicts.

When Max was around nine, like millions of others in this time period, he became Minecraft obsessed. I still see countless comments from parents on social media lamenting this game, but over time, I became quite delighted by his fixation. It didn't start that way. At first, it seemed negative and hostile; we heard a lot about how mean other kids were and how they were "griefing" (attacking) his base. Then he was incessantly telling us crafting recipes – *To make a flint and steel, you need one piece of flint in the middle bottom row, but first you need to...*

Eventually, he managed to get Emma to try Minecraft, and she liked it. Then they sucked me in. If you're familiar with the game, you know there are many pros and cons, which we can discuss another time. What I liked wasn't the game itself. What delighted me was seeing Max lead.

He was much more advanced than either Emma or I. He would save us when there were scary monsters. He'd show us how to build cool structures. Eventually he created a family server, and we built worlds together. Sometimes when I was traveling, we'd play together across time zones. It was one of the best connections we made.

In contemporary Western society, children have little meaningful responsibility. It's wonderful that they have the space to be children, yet many of them find it a bit empty, a bit like waiting for the movie to start. If we want them to grow to be responsible, to be leaders, to be changemakers, then they need opportunities to practice that. One of the greatest gifts we can give our children is to take their aspirations seriously and to give them space to lead. Not someday, but now.

Tools for Leadership

To help your child build internal leadership skills, try:

Join your child in their passion. Even if it's not something you necessarily enjoy, you may find delight in their excitement.

Create opportunities for your child to be in charge. It could be planning a day out; it could be building a Minecraft server. The content is irrelevant. The goal is letting them hold the power.

Obsess and expand. Way back when I was teaching, I heard psychologist Mel Levine say about supporting kids' learning: Help them obsess, then diversify the obsession, because that builds a neurological structure for learning to go deep.

Chapter 10:
The Cusp of Tomorrow
Wrapping Up Part III

Think about this moment. Wherever you are, whenever it is, this one moment is so rich. I'm writing these words in the mountains of Laos, editing work I wrote on the other side of the planet, to be shared around the world. So many different weathers at this one moment. So many languages. So many flavors and sights and sounds. All together – here, now. This one instant is bursting with possibility.

A few years ago, my family and I had the pleasure of sitting *zazen* (a form of Japanese Buddhist meditation) with a delightful monk. He's the fifth generation of monks in a 600-year-old temple, Shunkoin, in Myoshinji, Kyoto, and his son would be born soon. Sitting on the woven rice-straw tatami mats glowing in the morning sun, looking at the simple geometry of hand-cut wood framing the walls, watching the incense smoke curling around my ten-year-old son (in his bright orange signature colors), I was touched by the confluence of all these rivers coming together in that one moment. Kawakami-san, the monk, reminded us that every moment, the moment is passing. And as the moments pass, we may end up with fewer and fewer choices. Life is not a static experience, but one of continuous flow. A flow from myriad options of childhood, to fewer options as we age.

A few months later, we buried Max's favorite pet chicken, Puff. I tied a few of Puff's orange-gold feathers with a white ribbon, and gave them to Max. As the kids filled in the grave, Patty sang "The Red River Valley," which we last sang at Hank's funeral, and I was overflowing with this strange mix of feelings. Sorrow and loss, but also joy and appreciation. A stunning day in this glorious place we live – beautiful golden feathers in my lovely boy's hands, a boy gentle and caring enough to be completely in love with a soft fluffy bird. My immediate family together, but my extended family spread far and wide.

I thought of Kawakami's counsel, that just because life is constantly passing and flowing, we don't *have* to lose the choices if we stay more aware, more awake in the passing moments. My experience that day as a parent, and again today, is that letting myself feel the mix of emotions awakens something in me, not fighting against myself, not trying to hold still in the flowing current – but feeling it for what it is, opening to it, and learning from it.

I feel this incredible pride and honor in witnessing our children stride, and I feel sad too. It reminds me of when I was a teacher, and the first time my students were graduating, I just couldn't stop crying. One of the other teachers said, "You should be happy, this is what we've been working toward." I was happy, but happy and sad are not so far apart.

I feel so blessed, so lucky for the gift of being a daddy, by the abundance of love and meaning and hope in my life. I'm deeply grateful, yet I feel this strange paradox of the near-perfection of the moment, mixed with a sense of insecurity – of joy somehow slipping away into the past as I hesitantly step into an unknown future. I'm not sure how to reconcile this. How do I stay in love with the present, knowing it's already gone?

All these feelings stirring around, perhaps I could boil them down to this: *Am I living my life, or simply passing through it?*

Our parenting lives are full of moments that are challenging, others that are beautiful, and some, like Puff's funeral, that are both. In all this complexity, how do we whole-heartedly engage? How do we stay awake, learning, and growing along with our children? I hope the emotional intelligence model provides a framework to support you in this:

Know Yourself

Pause of a moment to tune in. Listen to your emotions as a source of wisdom. Remember that your feelings are data – not bad or good, just information and energy. Stay curious about your own reactions. Remember we're all practicing, notice yourself in the process.

Choose Yourself

Use more of the moments intentionally. You've reacted the old way a thousand times, try something new today. You've tried and succeeded, tried and failed, tried and muddled through... and today you have the gift of another opportunity to experiment.

Give Yourself

Remember that you're parenting for powerful, meaningful reasons. You are adding to your child's life, you are adding to the world – what is it you want to add? The emotions you foster, the choices you make, are ripples you're sending outward.

Then do the process again. Use the opportunities to be more aware, more intentional, more purposeful. Those fascinating, challenging children keep changing. They grow, and suddenly we need to grow too. It's exhausting, but it's also invigorating. While so many of our interactions are the mundane, *I've told you 7,346 times not to leave your coat on the floor when you walk in the door...* the reason these interactions matter is that our children also remind us of the biggest questions. *Why we love. Who we choose to be. How we grow.*

The emotions of the journey signal the significance. Whether it's utter delight or sheer exhaustion, our emotions are there to keep reminding us that this matters. So rather than pushing feelings aside, embrace them with your whole heart. A big feeling means, "Pay Attention! Something important is happening." While it might be more placid to live with fewer emotions, it would be like a feast without any seasoning. So as you continue on your adventure of parenting, I hope you find many feelings. Feelings to challenge you, to connect you, to help you pay attention – and feelings to inspire you to keep learning.

About the Author

I grew up in a family of scientists, and I used to find emotions to be scary and overwhelming. After university, I was a humanities teacher in a school culture where people talked openly about feelings – and I found myself challenged to stop "being the expert" and to learn to "be a person." When I started to notice and name feelings, my relationship with my students changed, and I decided I'd better learn more about how emotions work.

Now I'm the CEO of a nonprofit organization called Six Seconds. I feel privileged to lead a network of many thousands of educators and trainers and changemakers spreading EQ around the world. We are working toward the vision of a billion people practicing emotional intelligence.

Over the last 18 years of teaching people to teach emotional intelligence, I've worked with big organizations like FedEx and the United Nations and the U.S. Navy, and with amazing people in large and small organizations all over the planet. My basic message is that emotions are valuable if we can learn to use them. Emotions can help us be leaders worth following. I've written several books about that, first *At the Heart of Leadership*, then *Inside Change*, and most recently, *The Vital Organization*.

I travel a lot. On customs forms, it asks for "occupation," and I'm never sure what to write. I'm an author and a researcher. I'm a coach and trainer, a leader and a changemaker. I'm a son and a husband and a daddy. In the end, I write "educator," and for me it means all those roles in one.

Invitation: Virtual Book Club

You're invited to join readers and parent-educators from the Six Seconds network in an ongoing virtual book club.

Connect with us online: 6sec.org/whpclub

About the Publisher

Six Seconds is a global nonprofit organization supporting people to harness the power and wisdom of feelings to create positive change - everywhere, all the time.

We publish powerful models and tools based on current neuroscience research. Changemakers use these methods with businesses, schools, government agencies, nonprofits, and families to help people thrive. Six Seconds is a global network with offices and representatives in 25 countries and certified practitioners in over 100 nations.

Learn more about Six Seconds online:

www.6seconds.org